CONFEDERATE
GENERAL
LEONIDAS
POLK

CONFEDERATE
GENERAL

LEONIDAS POLK

LOUISIANA'S FIGHTING BISHOP

CHERYL H. WHITE, PhD

Charleston London
THE
History
PRESS

Published by The History Press
Charleston, SC 29403
www.historypress.net

Back cover photo of Mount Olivet Chapel courtesy of Robert Harwell, Diocese of
Western Louisiana.

First published 2013

Manufactured in the United States

ISBN 978.1.60949.737.8

Library of Congress CIP data applied for.

This book is dedicated to those in the Succession of the Historic Episcopate from Right Reverend Leonidas Polk, First Bishop of Louisiana

Diocese of Louisiana 1866–present:
Right Reverend Joseph Wilmer
Right Reverend John Nicholas Galleher
Right Reverend Davis Sessums
Right Reverend James Morris
Right Reverend John Long Jackson
Right Reverend Girault M. Jones
Right Reverend Iveson B. Noland
Right Reverend James B. Brown
Right Reverend Charles E. Jenkins III
Right Reverend Morris K. Thompson

Diocese of Western Louisiana (created in 1979):
Right Reverend Willis R. Henton
Right Reverend Robert J. Hargrove Jr.
Right Reverend D. Bruce MacPherson
Right Reverend Jacob W. Owensby

CONTENTS

Acknowledgements   9

1. The Controversy of Leonidas Polk   11
2. Early Life, Education and a Christian Calling   23
3. Farmer, Preacher, Missionary Bishop   33
4. Bishop Polk in Antebellum Louisiana   43
5. Louisiana Secession Politics, War and the Protestant
   Episcopal Church   55
6. Major General Leonidas Polk in the Mississippi Valley, 1861   67
7. In the Army of Tennessee and Conflict with Braxton Bragg:
   1862–63   81
8. The Death and Legacy of the Bishop-General   99

Notes   111
Bibliography   119
Index   123
About the Author   125

ACKNOWLEDGEMENTS

I have long wanted to write about Bishop-General Leonidas Polk, for at the heart of his story is a set of complex contradictions. It was interests in Christian history, Louisiana history and the historic episcopate that first drew me to Polk, and I remain convinced that we may never quite fully understand him. In many ways, he is a historian's dream—his corpus of personal papers remains largely intact, he was witness to major events in American history and numerous other primary sources document his life. However, Polk continues to defy complete transparency. He was a complex man of a complex age, and his legacy will doubtlessly continue to be reevaluated.

There are many people who contributed to this work. I am grateful for my family's support and love and especially for Paul White, who on Friday mornings would fill the bird feeders outside the windows of my favorite writing spot in the sunroom and bring me coffee.

To my dear friends and colleagues Dr. Helen Wise and Dr. Alexander Mikaberidze, who were always willing to patiently listen as I explored differing interpretations of the bishop-general, I owe hearty thanks. My friend and colleague Dr. Gary Joiner was an invaluable resource, not only for his fierce knowledge of the American Civil War but also for his willingness to read and critique these drafts. The entire editorial staff of The History Press in Charleston, South Carolina, has been a great joy and delight to work with, and I thank them for helping me through this process.

As a teaching historian today, I remain aware of the impact that educators have on future generations of this discipline. I am grateful to a former professor who is now both mentor and friend. Dr. Milton Finley, professor emeritus of history, continues to inspire me in my chosen academic field, even after over thirty years have passed since my undergraduate studies and I first walked into his classroom.

I offer many thanks and appreciation to the people of various church parishes in the Episcopal Diocese of Louisiana and the Episcopal Diocese of Western Louisiana, who helped with photographs and anecdotes of Polk. It would take a much larger volume of work to include them all. I have given photographic credit to those who assisted with important images, especially Bob Harwell. Further, I offer thanks to the library of the University of North Carolina and other historians who have written significant works on Leonidas Polk, but especially Glen Robins, whose work significantly influenced my approach to Polk's blend of religious southern nationalism.

To Bishop-General Leonidas Polk: thank you, friend, for sharing your life's story with me so that I might share it with others. I only hope I have appropriately honored your legacy here.

Chapter 1

THE CONTROVERSY OF LEONIDAS POLK

"Blessings on Friend and Foe Alike"

The life of Confederate general and first Episcopal bishop of Louisiana Leonidas Polk has been the subject of a few comprehensive biographical works. Among those, the most ambitious and detailed was the work of Polk's own son, William Mecklenburg Polk, who seems to have been determined to quickly cement the historical legacy of his father before the close of the nineteenth century. Because of the rather anomalous nature of Polk's life and dual career as both a bishop of the Episcopal Church and as a general in the Confederate army, scholars have frequently been drawn to his story. The majority of what biographers have written about Polk focuses heavily on his military career, contributing to the numerous volumes of scholarship that deal with American Civil War history.

The episcopate of Leonidas Polk has attracted considerably less attention, representing the aspect of his life that historians have examined only secondarily to his military career. Yet an exploration of Leonidas Polk as bishop is one that contributes much to an overall understanding of a complex and enigmatic figure who straddled two contradictory worlds with an apparent ease that seems almost incomprehensible. An examination of his interests and the causes to which he most committed his energy reveals much more about his political and military nature than his life as a bishop of the church. Polk had no hesitation about rushing headfirst into

Bishop Leonidas Polk. An anecdote often attributed to Polk is that he reconciled his positions of bishop and general by saying he would "wear the sword over the bishop's gown." The complexity of his persona rests on the apparent contradictions of his roles during the Civil War. *Courtesy of Library of Congress, Civil War Prints and Photographs Division, Washington, D.C.*

political controversies of his day (i.e., the cause of Southern secession), but interestingly, he did not share the same vigorous enthusiasm for engaging in theological disputes. Even when making a case for the independence of the diocese after Louisiana seceded from the United States in 1861, Polk framed his argument in distinctly secular and political terminology.

The relative lack of theological controversy attaching itself to Leonidas Polk is also an indication of the generally stable condition of Protestantism in the United States at the middle of the nineteenth century and, more specifically, within the Protestant Episcopal Church. Before being plunged into the political divide wrought by the Civil War, the most contentious disputes of American Episcopalians centered on high-church versus low-church elements as they related to the denomination's identity derived from Anglicanism. The contributions of Polk's tenure as missionary bishop of the Southwest and then as bishop of Louisiana are measured in the strength of the Episcopal presence across the antebellum South. In Louisiana, Episcopalians represented the first vibrant and lively non–Roman Catholic presence. In addition, his vision for what would become the University of the South (Sewanee) reflected his sincere dedication to the Episcopal identity in America and a determination to preserve it for future generations. One cannot help but speculate on what more he might have accomplished in his ministry in Louisiana had there been no Civil War.

Although little is known of the childhood of Leonidas Polk, the general facts of his adult life are not in question; indeed, Polk's own correspondence is autobiographical. The narrative of his actions as a wartime general is externally and firmly corroborated in the annals of American military history. The lengthy and impressive genealogy of the Polk family reaches back into seventeenth-century Scottish Presbyterian roots and reveals a strong genetic predisposition to both separatism and patriotism—both of which define the entire history of the Polk clan. Mostly un-churched in his early life, Polk's conversion to Christianity while enrolled as a cadet at West Point Military Academy is an event that is also remarkably documented in extant sources. From that point forward, the historical trail is easily followed through both church and military records, as Polk lived his life in full view within both spheres. There is no point at which the historian lacks for detail in answering the questions that begin with *who*, *when* and *where*. It is sometimes the *why* questions that can be problematic, and this may be especially true with attempting to understand Leonidas Polk.

As mentioned, there are notable biographies of Polk, appropriately comprehensive in nature and covering his life and career in more than adequate detail. Because the most prominent of these was written by his direct descendant, William Mecklenburg Polk, all future writers have drawn heavily from this work or used it as an initial point of introduction. Polk's position in the pantheon of Civil War history vacillates between that of capable and virtuous hero and that of an impetuous and arrogant incompetent. Historians of that conflict remain divided over the exact nature of the important strategic contributions (if any) made by Polk. As Glenn Robins pointed out in his 2006 work, *The Bishop of the Old South: The Ministry and Civil War Legacy of Leonidas Polk*, General Polk has lived on in the "myths and romanticized truths of the Lost Cause."[1] Assuredly, the early treatment of Polk in the chronicles of history created an unassailable image of a martyr-general, almost completely obscuring his work in the ministry of the church before the war erupted in 1861.

Any new look at Bishop-General Polk could hardly find anything extraordinarily fresh or innovative to add to the existing corpus of literature; therefore, the ambition of this work is self-limited. This is not an attempt to rewrite that which has already been written about the life of Leonidas Polk but, rather, to add to that literature by simply looking at him through a more localized lens using the historical backdrop of his episcopacy in Louisiana. After all, it was his calling to Christian ministry that diverted him from a planned military career, and yet it was a calling into military service that diverted him from ministry. In the end, Polk fused the two callings in a way that may have left each lacking. The call to each shares the commonality of Louisiana; his prestige in the state rested on his status as a bishop of the Protestant Episcopal Church. This position, as well as his preexisting friendships with Jefferson Davis and Albert Sidney Johnston, served as a springboard into the political and military divide of 1861.

Much of Polk's influence is documented in histories of the state, providing a regional framework from which to understand Polk's life and legacy more fully. While it is true that his military career took him throughout the South, Polk's largest Episcopal mission field was always in Louisiana. Throughout the state today, there are countless visible reminders of his presence, be it in place names like Fort Polk that honor his military legacy or written in the parish records of the numerous churches he planted during his tenure as bishop.

The entire landscape of Louisiana is dotted with his memory, for there are Episcopal church cornerstones bearing his fingerprints in places as diverse as St. John's in Thibodaux, Mount Olivet in Pineville, Trinity Church in Natchitoches and Church of the Holy Cross (St. Mark's) in Shreveport.

The Controversy of Leonidas Polk

Mount Olivet Chapel in Pineville, Louisiana. Bishop Polk laid the cornerstone of this chapel in 1859. The structure is representative of the many small Episcopal churches that Polk planted throughout the region. The chapel today has been restored to its original historic luster through vigorous historic preservation efforts of D. Bruce MacPherson, the third Episcopal bishop of western Louisiana. The building complex functions as the Diocesan House for the Diocese of Western Louisiana today, and Confederate war dead are also buried in its adjacent cemetery. *Photo by Robert Harwell, Communications Officer for the Diocese of Western Louisiana.*

He becomes much more compelling when this persona surfaces. From his radical views on evangelizing slaves to his fearless preaching amidst a rowdy mob on the river docks of Shreveport, Polk the bishop seems every bit as courageous a man as Polk the general. It is this aspect of Polk that invites the scholar's inevitable attempt to reconcile the evangelist bishop with the warrior general.

Therefore, this work seeks to more directly probe Polk's complexity by looking at him as both a religious and military figure. This approach requires confronting the difficulty posed by these two seemingly contradictory personae. How did a man of God, a priest by ordination and a bishop of the historic Apostolic Succession, reconcile his divine calling to the ministry with the sword of a general during one of the bloodiest times in American history? Polk summarized his decision to accept military command by saying

Current photograph of Church of the Holy Cross Episcopal in Shreveport, Louisiana (originally St. Mark's Episcopal Church). A community of Episcopalians was established early in Shreveport history by Bishop Polk, perhaps as early as 1839. An oft-repeated anecdote suggests that Bishop Polk actually held the first church services on the banks of the Red River in Shreveport, despite protests from a boisterous group of dockworkers. This current building was constructed in 1895, but the church still houses the original cornerstone laid by Polk in 1859. *Courtesy of Church of the Holy Cross, Reverend Mary Richard, Rector.*

only that it was "the duty next." Was it actually as simple as Polk is popularly quoted as saying: "I wear the sword over my bishop's gown"? These are difficult questions, to be sure. To avoid putting words into Polk's mouth, this work relies heavily on the words of the bishop-general himself, drawn from his personal papers and military records.

What can be gleaned from this historical record produces a fascinating composite image. Leonidas Polk baptized soldiers on the eve of bloody battles, administered last rites to those mortally wounded, gave comfort to families of the fallen and even presided at weddings of officers in the occasional joyous interludes from the realities of war. Yet as a general he gave orders to kill in the name of a cause that many today consider to have been most unholy. Anecdotes reveal that in Polk the general resided a courage that would honor his namesake of Spartan antiquity yet also an emotional vulnerability that led him to weep for the fallen and drove him to find church altars at which to pray following a long day of battle. His love of family, parishioners, soldiers and even the enemy is obvious in his own memoirs with a sincerity that cannot be questioned. Yet, like all great Greek heroes, Polk possessed a fatal character flaw. His was manifest in arrogance, accompanied by an apparent inability to accept criticism or take responsibility for his mistakes.

That Polk would have a genetic predisposition to the military is obviated in his family tradition going back many generations. However, it is notable that Leonidas Polk altered the tradition of the Polk men to pursue patriotic military service by adding the layer of a genuine Christian faith, so he was prepared to take a somewhat different path than his ancestors. It was a path also profoundly shaped by the sociology of the antebellum South—that such a sharply divided society would elevate a man above the moral controversies of the day is not surprising upon examination. In a culture that embraced slavery and saw the violence of a bloody civil war, Leonidas Polk became an archetype of just the right "soldier-saint" to provide moral stability in a visible sense.[2]

Historians bear the responsibility of maintaining a perspective that rightly recalls historical figures within the social norms that framed the times to which they belong. It serves no purpose to judge Leonidas Polk by present-century standards of religiosity and culture; therefore, to see him as a bishop of the Episcopal Church who simultaneously served as a major general for the Confederacy is not a stumbling block to understanding him. It is a challenging premise from which to begin, but Polk is not unlike many other figures of history who are also equally remarkable studies in contrast. Such is the chief focus of this examination of Polk's life.

The passage of time carries with it the promise that people and events of the past will inevitably be subject to ongoing revision and scrutiny as historians try to grapple with changing social norms framed in new cultural understanding. Presently there is a tendency to reevaluate the accomplishments and contributions of historical figures against a backdrop of modern constructs. Such reexamination is quite naturally driven by an acute awareness of what constitutes "right" and "wrong" by the standards of the current culture. Leonidas Polk is an example of a figure whose place in history makes his legacy amenable to this type of unfortunate scrutiny.

It is Polk's service for the Confederate States of America that has engendered some recent controversy, perhaps especially within the quarters of the Episcopal Church. In the past, the church has attempted to both respect his memory and reject the political positions for which he fought and ultimately died. This has proven to be a precarious balancing act and one that has increasingly posited a deep question regarding the legacy of man who unquestionably converted many to the faith, brought the first viable and lively Protestant presence to Louisiana and yet represents the politics of one of the darkest periods in American history. Given the historical framework and circumstances of his life, it is easy to understand the controversy surrounding him. Furthermore, it is apparent that the controversy is itself a subject of controversy, for it brings to the fore the question of the continued relevance of historical perspective. A review of the literature finds that assessment of the "fighting bishop" is mixed.

In the official program for the June 2006 General Convention of the Episcopal Church held in Columbus, Ohio, the University of the South published a full-page tribute to Leonidas Polk. The tribute praised Polk's accomplishments as both a bishop and a soldier, pointing out that he ultimately gave his life on the battlefield. The purpose of the tribute rested in the fact that during the course of that General Convention fell the day of the 142nd anniversary of Polk's death on Pine Mountain in Georgia (June 14, 1864). This tribute prompted sharp criticism from those within the Episcopal Church who believe that Polk's support of slavery severely limits the ability of that denomination to commemorate such a man.[3]

Such an assessment certainly characterizes the dilemma facing the Episcopal Church when confronted with honoring a missionary bishop of some considerable success but who also happened to be a Confederate general. This anecdote demonstrates that Bishop-General Leonidas Polk has the ability to continue to provoke deep emotional responses from the painful memories of a nation's divided past. At the same time, such a posture neglects the remembrance that this was also a man who contributed much to the advancement of Protestant Christianity and higher education by the standards of the age in which he lived. Leonidas Polk was a man of the nineteenth century, not the twenty-first. Much like the founding fathers of this nation who expressed the idea that "all men are endowed by their Creator with certain inalienable rights," while personally keeping slaves and doing little to change the status quo of slavery, Polk's place in history cannot be completely and fairly viewed through modern lenses.

Beyond any difficulty in reconciling Polk's military service with his role as a bishop in the church, there is the added challenge of reconciling him to the very nature of the conflict itself. For a bishop of the church to fight in combat was something incomprehensible to many, but for a bishop to advocate armed rebellion against lawfully constituted civil authority raises deeper questions regarding scriptural admonitions calling for obedience to government. The contradictions of the clerical collar and the bars of the general are entangled in the very theological debates that Polk often tried to avoid.

When viewed on a broader historical scale, Polk's decision to serve the Confederate cause does much to highlight the dilemma that clergy everywhere would have faced during that time. Whether serving the Federal Union or the Confederate States of America, men of the cloth universally deliberated over whether to preach pacifism or commit to the fight. Clergy could have easily found sufficient scriptural warrant for either position, drawing on either the righteousness of war depicted in the Old Testament histories or the pacifism perceived in stories of Jesus in the New Testament.

In fact, what might be more difficult to imagine is that Christian clergy could have been neutral or remained silent about the conflict while the chaos of civil war wrought death and destruction just beyond the safety of their churches. As the war raged on and invaded the heartland of the South, even church buildings were no longer safe havens, and therefore clergy found it more difficult to remain neutral when their congregations were burying its sons too young. There can be no doubt that the American Civil War posed a great challenge for institutional Christianity, as it struggled to find moral answers and simultaneously serve those on both sides of the conflict.

As for the heart and mind of the bishop-general, Polk seems to have believed that his own conscience was clear with regard to both the established status quo of Southern slavery and the violence of civil war. A well-documented story relates that following the Battle of Perryville in October 1862, Bishop Polk entered St. Philip's Episcopal Church in Harrodsburg, Kentucky, and asked that the bell be tolled in remembrance, saying, "Peace to the land and blessings on friend and foe alike."[4] Among the personal pages of the bishop can be found a letter he wrote to his brother, who was trapped in Vicksburg, Mississippi, during the siege of 1863. In the letter, Polk drew upon an analogy from the western Roman Empire by repudiating "the conduct of the Goths and Vandals from the north," saying further that "the Lord rewards them according to their works," and "I firmly believe that He will dispose of our case in the way that shall be best for us and all the world."[5] Whether or not Polk envisioned an outcome that did not include a Confederate victory can only be the subject of speculation. All indications are that he believed in the justness of the Confederate cause and saw no contradiction to his work as a shepherd of Christ's flock. This is precisely the image of the "fighting bishop" that attracts historical reassessment and contributes to what will most likely be an ongoing controversy regarding his overall legacy.

A cursory examination of medieval history produces evidence that the concept of a bishop as a true Christian soldier has often existed in Christianity. In addition to the examples of the warrior-bishops of the Carolingian era, there is also the story of Odo, the eleventh-century bishop of Bayeux and half brother to William the Conqueror, who was present at the Battle of Hastings. There is another such bishop-general to be found in Archbishop Albero of Trier in the twelfth century. Medieval Christianity intersected with the violent and turbulent era of the Crusades that popularized the iconic imagery of the Christian soldier, so these examples are not at all surprising.

There is also significant historical symbolism to help illuminate the complexities posed by a bishop riding at the head of an army, even up to the point of arguing secession politics in nineteenth-century America. In the fourteenth century, a pope named Boniface VIII wrote of two swords, one spiritual and one temporal, both wielded by the church and representing the swords of the Apostles at the arrest of Christ. To the medieval mind, the secular sword was wielded by the church as a reminder of the proper order—that civil authority was secondary to spiritual authority. When civil authority acted incorrectly, it was to be set right by the spiritual power of the first sword. The medieval church understood this to be of divine origin and commission, and such rhetoric framed the debates in church-state relations for centuries.

From the time of the early Christian fathers, the crosier, or bishop's staff, represented the pastoral nature of that same church authority. Metaphorically or actually, it was the symbol of the shepherd of the flock of God. In the secular affairs of civil governments, the church wielded a corrective sword; in pastoral matters affecting the community of the faithful, the church offered the gentle crook of a shepherd. Although one can never be certain that Polk ever delved into the theological implications of his concurrent earthly offices, there is something about these images from ecclesiastical history that resonates with his tale.

For Leonidas Polk, the sword and the crosier were both visible symbols of his life and work, and he employed each of them in ways that posed no apparent contradiction for him. His battlefields may have numbered more than his mission fields, but it was the mission field that witnessed Polk's most dramatic and unassailable achievements. His significant contributions to · the religious culture of the South, particularly in Louisiana, result from his evangelism efforts while serving as Episcopal bishop of Louisiana. No such dramatic claims can be made from exposing his military command to the same historical scrutiny, for his detractors are quick to point out Polk's lack of ability and his serial insubordination. Polk had a tendency to disobey orders from those higher in the Confederate command structure, and he always justified this with his superior firsthand knowledge of any given situation. In fact, without the friendship of Confederate president Jefferson Davis, Polk faced an almost-certain court-martial and possible disgrace by 1863.

To explore one aspect of Polk (the general) without balancing the other (the bishop) not only ignores the sum of the man but also makes the assessment of his true historical legacy more challenging than it ought to be. While the military historian either lauds or criticizes Polk's actions as a general, the social and religious historian can only laud his stature as a progressive visionary of Christianity in the nineteenth century. Therefore, one should enter the story of Bishop-General Leonidas Polk with an eye on the crosier as well as the sword.

Chapter 2

EARLY LIFE, EDUCATION AND A CHRISTIAN CALLING

"I Am Fully Persuaded"

O n the tenth day of April 1806, William and Sarah Polk of Raleigh, North Carolina, welcomed into the world a son they named Leonidas, derived from the Greek *leon* or lion. The Polks' name selection for their son is nothing short of prophetic, for a quick survey of history reveals two rather famous examples. Previous biographers have made much of the fact that Leonidas was a great Spartan warrior of antiquity who, with a courageous army of three hundred, stood against a massive Persian invasion at the famous Battle of Thermopylae. This is unquestionably the Leonidas of history whom William Polk had in mind when he named his second son, but there is yet another example from ancient Greece—that of Leonidas, a bishop of the third-century Christian church in Athens, who suffered martyrdom in Corinth. It is no small irony that this namesake, this Leonidas Polk of North Carolina, grew up to be both warrior and bishop in a war-torn landscape many centuries removed from those men of classical antiquity.

The claim that Leonidas Polk could trace his ancestry back to the Pollock clan of Scotland who settled in Ireland in the seventeenth century is not without its detractors, but if true, it explains much about the Polk family of nineteenth-century North Carolina. Many biographers have placed the origin of the family near Glasgow, with a migration to Donegal, Ireland, during the reign of James I (1603–1625).[6] These Pollocks would have been from strongly independent Scottish Presbyterian roots and could not have been indifferent to the divisive religious reform movements of the British Isles at that point in time. Scottish Presbyterians would have sympathized and aligned with Oliver Cromwell's revolution against church and monarchy that was the English Civil War. According to family tradition, one Robert Pollock served in Ireland under Cromwell and then migrated to Maryland, shortly thereafter changing the family name to Polk.[7]

Such a lineage would mean a peculiarly separatist genetic code for the Polk family, who, upon finding themselves against the backdrop of a brewing American Revolutionary War, would once again be in the role of rebel Patriots. Thomas Polk, the grandfather of Leonidas, moved in 1753 to Mecklenburg County, North Carolina, where he prospered as a planter. His marriage to Susanna Sprat produced eight children, including William Polk, Leonidas's father. Thomas Polk made his personal politics well known as a signatory of the Mecklenburg Declaration of 1775, which purportedly advocated separation from Great Britain and the establishment of an autonomous local government.[8]

Thomas Polk may have been among the first proponents of full independence from Britain, making him rather unusual among fellow planters in the South at the time. The general sentiment in the early stages of the conflict seems to have rested on the notion that to have Britain address the grievances of colonists would be sufficient. The majority of colonists in North America had come from Britain; therefore, they were people who understood principles of liberty. The neglect with which Britain had treated the colonists while preoccupied with wars of trade rivalry in the first half of the eighteenth century did much to damage the sense of shared identity between colonies and mother country. When the Revolutionary conflict began, Thomas Polk took a commission in the North Carolina regiments being formed against Great Britain. He served with distinction under General Francis Nash in the Philadelphia Campaign and suffered great personal disappointment at not being elevated upon the death of Nash in October 1777 during the Battle of Germantown.[9]

Thomas Polk continued in his commitment to the cause of independence, in spite of his disappointment and lack of confidence in its generals; both George Washington and Horatio Gates were subjects of Polk's criticism. Yet he returned to battle under the command of Nathanael Greene during the skirmish at Rugeley's Mill in South Carolina in 1780, after which Thomas Polk earned the rank of general.[10] Furthermore, Thomas Polk's use of his personal credit as guarantee of military debts is a fact well documented in his correspondence with General Greene. The Polks were quite literally willing to back the cause of colonial independence with their personal resources, which is an attestation to the family's commitment to patriotism.

William Polk, son of Thomas and father of Leonidas, is also distinguished in Revolutionary War history, enlisting to fight on the side of the colonists alongside his father at the age of seventeen. At the age of eighteen, he ranked as a major and commanded a regiment. He was wounded in October 1777 and spent the harsh winter with General Washington quartered at Valley Forge. Therefore, the Polk men had a reputation for courage and commitment, but William added celebrity as well because of his association with the Marquis de Lafayette. Lafayette visited North Carolina in 1825, and William Polk served as part of the welcoming party and publicly rejoined himself to the respected Frenchman. It was still an age when the republican principles of the Revolutionary era inspired awe among the common people, and the Polk family seemed to exude those values. Lafayette was a hero in the American patriotic hall of fame who symbolized ideals that Americans yet related to a half century after independence.[11] The Polk family stature elevated considerably as a result of this association.

By the end of the war, William Polk held the rank of colonel and served in the North Carolina assembly as a representative from Mecklenburg. President Washington appointed him as supervisor of internal revenue for North Carolina, and he held this post for several years. The family found further distinction with the relation of James K. Polk, a cousin, who became U.S. president in 1845 after serving as Speaker of the House of Representatives and governor of Tennessee. It was into this family steeped in patriotism and genealogical virtue that Leonidas Polk was born.

Little is known about the early years of Leonidas Polk—only what one can infer about the social conditions and expectations of nineteenth-century southern aristocracy. There is no reason to think that what was normative for this distinct class of the antebellum South would not have applied to the young Leonidas Polk. He appears to have been mostly un-churched as a child and adolescent, if his self-proclaimed conversion to Christianity as an adult is any indication. The majority of the North Carolina planter aristocracy would have self-identified as Episcopalians, but this cannot be said of the Polks. Leonidas's father seems to have held a moderate amount of disdain for all organized religion and traditional Christian doctrines.[12] An example of this is documented in an often-repeated anecdote involving the Episcopal bishop of North Carolina, John Ravenscroft, a man who himself earned a descriptive nickname and distinctive reputation by the standards of the age, being known as both "Mad Jack" and "the most unconventional man in the House of Bishops."[13]

In a way that must have impacted the religious development of his own children, William Polk personally rejected traditional Christian teachings of the atonement, instead promoting his belief that it was the measure of a man's moral character that assured individual salvation. The view indicates the elder Polk might have inherited an exposure or influence from Enlightenment deism, which would have been popular with a certain quarter of the southern aristocracy of the late eighteenth century. Bishop Ravenscroft, in a personal exchange with the elder Polk, responded that a man holding such heretical views "would go straight to hell."[14] This anecdote illustrates yet another manifestation of the strong independent spirit of the Polk clan, in this case by rejecting the traditional doctrinal orthodoxy of Christianity as held by the majority of the landed class by this time in American history. All of this likely made an impression on the young Leonidas, but the influence of Bishop Ravenscroft was not complete. It was Ravenscroft who confirmed Leonidas at Christ Church in Raleigh, North Carolina, in 1827.[15]

Leonidas entered the University of North Carolina in 1821, and of his time there, one especially poignant letter has survived that provides some insight to the profound bonds of familial affection, tempered with a bit of homesickness from the young man. To his sister Mary, Leonidas wrote, "You have no conception of the pleasure I derive from the perusal of a letter from you, being so far distant from home."[16] Love and respect for family were constant themes in the life of Leonidas Polk, evidenced repeatedly in the surviving corpus of letters.

While enrolled in his studies at Chapel Hill, Leonidas received an appointment to the United States Military Academy at West Point and expressed his thrill at the news in a letter to his father on March 10, 1823: "You can imagine but few thing which have more highly gratified me…I hailed it with delight as the messenger bearing tiding of an appointment so long wished for."[17] Indeed, it was both the fulfillment of an expectation and an indication that social obligations were directly on course, for young aristocratic men of the South studied at West Point.

Polk entered West Point at a time when the school was reaching a peak of efficiency and prestige under the leadership of Sylvanus Thayer. The methods, curriculum and discipline that are the mark of the academy today are largely the work of this man.[18] Cadets knew Thayer to be a man of strict but fair discipline, impeccably disciplined himself in both manner and habits. One of Thayer's reforms was the practice of abolishing summer vacations for the cadets, substituting instead a summer encampment. During this time, cadets were required to live in tents as soldiers and practice maneuvers.[19] This aspect of academy life seemed to thrill Leonidas Polk.

His life at West Point as a young cadet was chronicled by Leonidas's son, William Mecklenburg Polk, in an early biography that is perhaps not an unbiased source. According to that account, Leonidas often incurred the "displeasure of his superiors at the Academy, but only because he demanded a level of obedience that few could match."[20] Polk was often at the receiving end of Thayer's discipline, and it seems to have created some resentment in the young cadet. One such conflict with Thayer during examinations in early 1826 resulted in the lowering of Polk's standing in the class. Leonidas wrote hastily to his father to explain: "I feel it incumbent on me to state that it is as unjust as it is injurious."[21] As later historians have analyzed Leonidas Polk, the difficulties at West Point can be interpreted as an early indicator of his inflexibility and, later, an unwillingness to follow orders. In the young cadet, there are indicators that Polk was certain of his own inerrancy.

A significant and historic close friendship formed at West Point was that of Albert Sidney Johnston, who was an upperclassman when Polk arrived. The two men became roommates until Johnston graduated in 1826. Perhaps because of Johnston's friendship, Polk earned the rank of sergeant major, which was the highest-ranking office among cadets.[22] The correspondence between Leonidas and William Polk during this period reveals a young man anxious to prove his military ability and a clear intent to please his father.

What also seems clear from the record is that while a cadet at West Point, Leonidas Polk had occasional disagreements with fellow cadets and with faculty, which may have contributed to his serious countenance and brooding, character traits that have attracted the commentary of most of his biographers. Perhaps because of this aspect of his personality, it appears that a newly arrived academy chaplain, Dr. Charles Pettit McIlvaine (the future Episcopal bishop of Ohio), arranged for a religious tract to be placed in Polk's dormitory, perhaps with the hope that it could offer some measure of solace. It was a turning point in the life of Leonidas Polk, and even Jefferson Davis mentioned in his final memoirs that Polk was converted to Christianity while at West Point and directly credited McIlvaine's influence in the future events of Polk's life.[23]

McIlvaine remembered Polk, Johnston, Davis and their classmates in his own correspondence during the Civil War, musing on what had become of those young men now in military service, noting them as "attendants to my ministry."[24] McIlvaine's description of his chaplaincy at the academy reveals an environment where religious faith was not openly discussed

Charles Pettit McIlvaine, chaplain at West Point Military Academy and Episcopal bishop of Ohio. McIlvaine baptized Polk while he was enrolled as a cadet at West Point Military Academy, an event McIlvaine recalled fondly in later memoirs following Polk's death in the war. *Courtesy of Library of Congress, Civil War Prints and Photographs Division, Washington, D.C.*

and regulations discouraged cadets from seeking him out for counsel or instruction.[25] McIlvaine described it thus: "I had been laboring for nearly a year without the slightest encouragement. Not a cadet had called to see me…they seemed to feel it would be regarded as a profession of interest in religion to come to me."[26] In spite of those conditions, Leonidas Polk responded to McIlvaine's outreach and became a converted Christian in the cadet corps. The chaplain's recollection of their first meeting is recorded: "He [Polk] burst into the most feeling and intense expression of a mind convinced of sin, and earnestly begged me to be told what he must do for salvation."[27]

In 1872, McIlvaine wrote what would be his final letter to General Sylvanus Thayer ("the Father of West Point"). In it, McIlvaine, by then the Episcopal bishop of Ohio, made reference to Polk's conversion as an aside:

> *By the way, do you remember the scene of the baptism of Cadet Polk in the chapel, and my having made a address to him…and how, in response to some charge to be faithful, he broke out with a deep "Amen" as if it came from de profundis? Well, after he was killed, I had a letter from a gentleman of Pennsylvania, a stranger, saying that on a certain Sunday he was stopping at West Point, and went to church as I baptized two cadets; and he remembered still my address almost in its words, and he recollected how he was impressed with the* Amen *of one of the baptized; that he had never lost the impression; that on hearing of Polk's death, it struck him that such was the name of the cadet, and he wrote me to inquire if it was so.*[28]

Polk was indeed baptized in the chapel at West Point in 1826, and in his newfound faith of Christianity, he began to experience doubt about pursuing a life as a soldier. When he wrote home to his father about his profound conversion experience, the tempered response from William Polk was cautionary, urging his son not to be caught up in "momentary enthusiasm."[29] Still, Leonidas felt a calling to ministry, especially throughout his final year at West Point. His father, clearly angered and frustrated with this turn of events, asked that Leonidas postpone his decision until after graduation.[30]

As for Chaplain McIlvaine, although initially discouraged by his post at West Point, he saw some change in the corps environment after Polk's conversion: "It pleased God that this, although the first, was not the only instance. Cadets and officers afterwards told me that I had chosen one man out of the whole corps, whose example would have the greatest effect on the minds of his comrades, I should have chosen him [Polk]."[31]

This was a development that Leonidas also proudly noted in a letter home: "Since I have entered unto my new, and I earnestly hope permanent, course of life, six others of the corps have successively come forward after the same manner, and we hope for a further increase."[32]

Although Polk unquestionably regretted the disappointment these developments caused his father, his correspondence continued to reflect the palpable respect and affection always present in their earlier relationship. Polk's own words reveal a need to demonstrate to his father that the decision was the result of a rigorous and disciplined approach to discernment. He wrote his father regarding his intention to enter the ordained ministry: "I have repeatedly surveyed the whole field of human avocation to find out that course which interest and inclination should direct me to proceed, and I am happy in being able to pronounce my search has not been fruitless...I am fully persuaded that the ministry is the profession to which I should devote myself."[33]

Polk's final examinations at West Point reflect a record of reversal of his misfortunes of the previous year, with a final ranking of eighth on the merit roll.[34] In the summer of 1827, he traveled throughout Canada and New England, finally arriving in Tennessee by October of that year. Polk's decision to forego immediate use of his training at West Point and a military career by entering the ordained ministry of the Episcopal Church was not without some personal sense of grief and sacrifice. He knew it was a disappointment to his parents; the Polk family of North Carolina reflected a lengthy genealogy of proud and patriotic military service. Yet Leonidas Polk, named for the great warrior Spartan king of antiquity, descended from distinguished Revolutionary soldiers, began his studies for ministry at the newly constituted Virginia Theological Seminary in November 1828.[35]

At Virginia Theological, Polk quickly earned the respect of fellow students in an environment where he seemed to simply transfer the military obedience of the West Point experience to the seminary. In fact, many contemporaries considered Polk to be among the most distinguished graduates of the seminary during its first years of existence.[36] This is despite the poor assessment of Polk's academic work given by William Mecklenburg Polk in his early biography, which notes that "he made no attempt to make up for the disadvantage of a lack of a classical education...his studies in ecclesiastical history were meager."[37] From the outset, however, he appeared to be an enthusiastic evangelical known for sharp criticism of Calvinism and a devotee to the Gospel he first heard from McIlvaine. He maintained an almost continual correspondence with his father during the time of his theological study and seems to have tried to avoid with his father any discussion of seminary. Their correspondence was instead full of the political news of the day—chiefly, that surrounding Andrew Jackson and the spoils system.[38]

Polk soon married his childhood sweetheart, Frances Devereaux in May 1830, just one month after his ordination as deacon in Richmond.[39] He was then ordained a priest in May 1831 in Norfolk, Virginia, just a few months after the birth of a son, Hamilton Polk (named for Leonidas's brother Hamilton, who had died of tuberculosis the year before).[40] A life of Christian ministry and a new family had begun, and the days at West Point with plans of becoming a soldier must have seemed far behind him. He could not have known then how future national events would resurrect his military interests and training in the future.

Chapter 3

FARMER, PREACHER, MISSIONARY BISHOP

"I Came Out Here for an Active Life"

B eginning with his conversion experience, the life of Leonidas Polk can be said to have ultimately rested between two worlds—that of the Protestant Episcopal Church[41] and that of the Confederate States of America. The story of the Episcopal Church in American history is inextricably bound to the story of English colonization of the New World and therefore has profound compatibility with the ideals of the same early American republic for which Polk's ancestors willingly fought. The faith tradition of Leonidas Polk also bore the identity of separation, an intellectual underpinning that would resurface during the hostilities of the Civil War.

From the time that Sir Francis Drake read a service of Morning Prayer from the Book of Common Prayer in what is today San Francisco Bay to the founding of Jamestown in Virginia, the loyal English presence in the New World sought only to replicate the expression of Christianity it had inherited. Jamestown attempted to simply transplant the local parish church from England into the wilderness of Virginia, and from 1607 onward, the Anglican presence in North America was assured. From 48 parish churches in Virginia recorded in 1671 to 107 by the time of American independence, the Church of England grew steadily, if not rapidly.[42]

So successful was the English colonial subjects' self-identification with the Church of England that they found themselves at a distinct cultural disadvantage, to say nothing of the inherent political disadvantage. These were people who understood the episcopacy as a model of church governance and accepted it unquestioningly as it had been handed to them by centuries of tradition. Unfortunately for the English colonists, the promised Episcopal oversight of those transplanted faith communities rested with the bishop of London, remote and distant as he was. Pleas for a bishop for the colonies fell on deaf ears across the Atlantic Ocean. The Church of England presence in North America suffered the same lack of attention as political oversight of the colonies did, until such time that the "American" identity grew over generations to be beyond the reach of the "English" identity with which the colonies began their existence. The fact that other Christian expressions existed in the colonies without need of an Episcopal structure put these Church of Englanders at another disadvantage both culturally and socially and, finally, politically, as the matriarchal strains of church and Crown became linked during the Revolutionary War.

It was upon the Church of England in the colonies that the consequences of the Revolution were most immediately and sharply felt. Many laypeople might have chosen between Crown and prayer book; the same freedom of choice did not naturally extend to the clergy, whose ordination vows bound them to the king. This was an oath that many clergy could not put aside in exercise of good conscience. Some clergy left to return to England while others simply left their parish churches to find other means of living, but both of these scenarios left Anglican parishioners with vacant pulpits and no reliable access to the Sacraments.[43]

The aftermath of the Revolutionary War brought even worse conditions for Church of England adherents in the new United States, for their faith expression was that of English aristocrats and the Crown, not of the self-made independent "Americans" who fought the established order (which would have included the Church of England as a national church). The post–Revolutionary War Church of England was disestablished, defunct and in complete disorder.[44]

Through this interesting confluence of history, the Episcopal Church and the United States were born at the same time under similar circumstances. Inevitably, the identities of the two would be intellectually similar and linked; both drew upon egalitarian ideals of governance models born of the Enlightenment. The constitution of the Episcopal Church provided bishops with separate and identified powers and a significant place for the laity in the life of the church and adopted the English Book of Common Prayer with only minor changes. By the early nineteenth century, the Protestant

Episcopal Church had bishops in seven of thirteen states.[45] Apparently, many people in the early American republic believed that this attempt at continuing the Church of England was pointless and unsustainable. Bishop William White of Pennsylvania alluded to this reality when he acknowledged, "The congregations of our communion were approaching annihilation."[46]

While Virginia always had claim to a strong Anglican presence, Polk's home of North Carolina did not. There, the established Church of England has a chaotic history at best. David Holmes reports that in 1765, there were thirty-two Anglican parishes there, yet only five of them were served by priests. The Anglican presence there seems to have suffered from the unique demographics of the laity, with too few interested in committing to the ongoing support that local parish churches needed in order to survive and thrive.[47]

In other areas, this static condition continued into the nineteenth century; it is this status of the Episcopal Church that prompted church leaders to begin discussion about missionary efforts elsewhere, beyond the boundaries of what had been historically considered English America. There was such a request discussed at General Convention in 1811, but nothing further happened until 1835 with Polk's appointment. In this move, the church moved into its own rather revolutionary mode of thinking—that its role in America could be missionary and evangelical in its scope. The old-guard New Englanders and Crown Loyalists accepted that a growing republic meant infusing new life if the Anglican presence in North America was going to live out the century.[48]

This transition period in the life of the Episcopal Church meant there would naturally be efforts to hang onto the English identity. The high-church party emphasized the episcopacy and identity with the Church of England as a historical tether. As a counterweight emerged the low-church party, which emphasized less ritual and identification with the past and more zeal attached to growing the numbers of the church. Therefore, the low-church element came to include those who labeled themselves "evangelicals," a party that Leonidas Polk identified with. Polk soon enough set himself to the task of missionary evangelism of this uniquely American expression of Anglican Christianity.

With the new year of 1831, Leonidas Polk found himself a new father and a new priest. However, he was also suffering with some nature of prolonged ill health, which many believed to be the same consumption (tuberculosis) that had claimed the life of his brother. He sought medical advice from a noted physician in Philadelphia who pronounced Polk to be quite near death. As a possible cure, Polk was encouraged to undertake a journey to Europe for a change of environment, and he departed the United States in August 1831 for Paris. There, his health gradually improved, and he traveled through Switzerland to Italy and spent several weeks in Rome. He then journeyed on to Naples, Nice and back to Marseilles, Lyons and finally Paris by early 1832, where he found a city in the midst of a devastating cholera epidemic, to which he also fell victim. Upon recovery from that illness, Polk traveled to England, where he spent much of 1832 enjoying the English countryside and learning about the Church of England. Polk did not return home to the United States until the end of that year.[49]

Polk's bouts with illness are probably what drove him to desire a rural lifestyle, believing it healthier than the urban environs he now associated with a near-death experience. In April 1833, the Polks set out for Maury County, Tennessee, where brother Lucius Polk already resided. Leonidas's letters home reflect that he immediately took to the farm lifestyle and was filled with enthusiasm for the daily work to be done. To his mother in August 1833 he wrote, "I find that to look after one's farm, and superintend all the various arrangements necessary to building, is no small task; but I came out here for an active life, and it is well I am not disappointed."[50]

Polk's father died in early 1834, and although Leonidas was not actively engaged in ministry at the time, his correspondence to his mother provides insight into the profound nature of his personal faith. "We are not left comfortless or without hope," Polk wrote lovingly. "With God, who was the author of the qualities which distinguished him, and who has ever vouchsafed mercy to the humble and the penitent, we may confidently leave him."[51] The death of his father may have indeed been a major turning point, as was his move to Tennessee. It was a time when a significant relationship took root with James Hervey Otey, bishop of the newly constituted Diocese of Tennessee. It was Otey who persuaded Polk to take on the duty of rector at St. Peter's Church in Columbia, Tennessee. Since there were not many Episcopalians in Tennessee at the time, Polk probably believed the assignment would allow him to continue what seems to have still been his chief occupation—plantation farming.[52] However, this active ministry role did much to place him back in the purview of established church leadership. It was Bishop Otey who drew Polk into the sphere of Episcopal Church policy, with Polk even serving as a delegate to the General Convention in 1835.[53]

Bishop Otey favored high-church Anglicanism,[54] but that did not mean he had no evangelical sympathies, and he may have identified in Polk a characteristic that balanced his own views. Otey believed the social order of America must embrace Christian values and therefore saw the nonnegotiable necessity of missionary efforts.[55] In 1838, the General Convention of the Episcopal Church met and appointed Leonidas Polk to become the new missionary bishop of the Southwest.[56] The sparse nature of the historical record indicates only that Polk was not the first choice for the task, and due to the lack of written record, historians have assumed that it was Otey who promoted the appointment of his friend Leonidas Polk to the office. Polk's absence at the 1838 General Convention brings into question how much he may have even known about the appointment in advance.[57] One thing was certain— Polk became missionary bishop to a vast wilderness where the Episcopal Church

Leonidas Polk, 1852. Polk's decision to defer a military career and instead enter ordained ministry represented a departure from a long-standing Polk family tradition of patriotic service. *Courtesy of Library of Congress, Washington, D.C.*

was an unknown, for the territory of his new mission field covered much of what is today part of Texas, Arkansas, Oklahoma (Indian Territory, as it was known), Louisiana, Mississippi and Alabama.

In 1835, the General Convention of the Protestant Episcopal Church decided to make domestic missions a priority by charging the entire church with responsibility for such endeavors. The decision to create missionary districts and send bishops into those regions before any Episcopal communities existed was a bold one, perhaps modeled on the earliest churches described in *Acts of the Apostles*. The first such missionary bishop was Jackson Kemper that same year. The large size of these missionary regions meant that bishops spent more time traveling than in any other effort, and the lack of financial support for their work meant that men assuming this charge would have to have other means of sustenance.[58] Yet there were men who responded to this tall order of the Protestant Episcopal Church, including Leonidas Polk.

Polk's biographers have noted that his response to the church was that of a soldier taking orders; he simply obeyed the call as if it had all the markers of a general's instructions. It is remarkable that he responded with this military-style obedience, for the previous decade of his life had been characterized by a seeming lack of true direction. It had been a time when Polk traveled extensively, always comfortably relying on the funding of his father and the ability of his father to introduce him to noted individuals. In his younger days, he had rubbed elbows with Martin van Buren and Andrew Jackson; after leaving West Point, he dined with John Quincy Adams and Henry Clay. Politics always seemed to be the most constant interest of Polk, and the genuine fervor of his Christian conversion did not initially seem to inspire his public ministry. During the intervening years between his ordination and his elevation to the episcopacy, Polk's attention seemed to wander from travel to farming and family life but never settled on the task of the ministry to which he was sure he had received a divine calling. How much of this inattention and lack of focus can be attributed to bouts of intermittent illnesses is uncertain, but clearly Polk's poor health in his early twenties must have been a factor.

However, when the appointment came from the Episcopal Church, Leonidas Polk accepted the challenge of shouldering the historic episcopate in what was still a huge American wilderness with an unbridled enthusiasm that is obvious in the documented record. On December 9, 1838, Polk was consecrated bishop in Cincinnati, and the sermon for the event was given by his dear mentor McIlvaine, who used the opportunity to recount for all present the conversion of Cadet Leonidas Polk at West Point Military Academy. The event was a fusion of both unique aspects of this complex man. Military cadet, deacon, priest and, finally, bishop, Leonidas Polk viewed all as a natural progression of God's will but a progression that unquestionably synthesized soldier and pastor.

As a soldier who leaves with orders, Polk left behind his home and family to take on the responsibilities of shepherd in an enormous field with a diverse population. For approximately six months, Polk traveled through both swamps and forests to preach and baptize. Beginning in Alabama and Mississippi, Polk worked his way into Arkansas and then Louisiana. In that brief period of time, Polk is credited with forty-four sermons, fourteen baptisms, forty-one confirmations, the consecration of one parish church and overseeing the laying of the cornerstone of another. He did this while covering five thousand miles on horseback or foot.[59] The cadet bishop had a true focus, a mission and statistics that indicated his work was bearing fruit in a measurable way.

The Episcopal Church of the nineteenth century appealed more to wealthy landowners than to simple planters. The denomination's history and dignified liturgy resonated with an educated elite who might have been reared in the Calvinist traditions that first characterized early colonial settlements but who found beauty in the tradition. The simultaneous influence of Romanticism likely did much to contribute to the denomination's appeal in this way. Even the church's success among the elite served as a means of attracting more adherents.

Yet for the most part, Polk's mission field was untamed wilderness. This may have been particularly true in the state of Louisiana, dominated by its rivers, bays and bayous. The Mississippi River and the Red River both served as major highways of transport, and each contributed to the fertility of Louisiana soil. Farther south are some of the world's most impressive wetlands. The region always boasted a productive agricultural economy. Polk's success in extending the influence of the Protestant Episcopal Church in such circumstances becomes more remarkable.

In 1841, Polk purchased a sugar plantation near modern-day Thibodaux in south Louisiana, placing him closer to his Episcopal jurisdiction in a way that would simultaneously nurture his love of farming. Shortly after this, he learned of his election as bishop of the new diocese of Louisiana, constituted precisely because of his successful efforts in planting an Episcopal presence in the region.[60] His brother Lucius assisted with the purchase of Leighton Plantation, seeing the obvious investment value at this time in history. Sugar planting was booming as an industry in Louisiana, and both the Polk brothers were interested in riding the tide of sugar's success, apparently undaunted by the challenge. Sugar required more capital and more investment in mechanization than any other crop grown at the time in the United States,[61] to say nothing of the labor-intensive nature of the enterprise. It was an age when planters grew sugar all along the fertile banks of the Mississippi River but especially near Bayou Lafourche. This was because here was the rare bit of high land in southern Louisiana.

Sources vary on estimates, but Louisiana produced as much as 95 percent of the sugar in the antebellum period in the South. The time that Polk was a sugar planter, from 1841 until the early 1850s, witnessed the economic boom of sugar. The industry took a dramatic turn in the nineteenth century, made possible only because of unique conditions. The historical intersection of steam technology, processing innovations and slave labor served to strengthen sugar's place as the dominant Louisiana crop of the century.[62]

The climate of Louisiana is not quite tropical, for in true tropical environs, sugar is grown for a year before harvest. At best, Louisiana could stretch a nine-month growing period, so it would require the innovations of making granulated sugar from cane juice to produce the sugar boom. With the amount

Workers harvesting sugar cane in Louisiana, circa 1880. This photograph was the creation of photographer William Henry Jackson, who captured images of late nineteenth-century life in Louisiana. Although taken three decades after Polk's life as a sugar planter, this image nevertheless depicts a realistic view of the labor-intensive nature of the crop. *Courtesy of Library of Congress, Prints and Photographs Division, Washington, D.C.*

of sugar produced in Louisiana, sugar planters were a powerful group; they were protected from Caribbean competition by high tariffs, and sugar soon supplanted cotton as the major cash crop of the state.[63] This was the economic state at the time of Polk's purchase of Leighton Plantation in 1841.

Among Louisiana's sugar cane plantations of note, Leighton was a top producer.[64] However, an 1849 cholera epidemic claimed large numbers of slaves on the Polk plantation, and sugar production waned over the next few years. Records indicate Polk was able to recover from initial financial losses attributable to both the cholera outbreak and personal property damages from a storm in 1851.[65] In private papers, Mrs. Polk noted of this, "The cholera appeared in our neighborhood in the winter of 1848–49. Great pains were taken by my husband to preserve the health of the negroes by clothing them in flannel and having their quarters under extraordinary police and sanitary regulations."[66]

Mrs. Polk went on to note that her husband also fell ill with the disease after traveling to preside over the diocesan convention but that his recovery was marked by an immediate return to his pastoral duties: "As soon as the bishop was able, indeed, at a risk of a relapse—he was at the bedside of the sick and dying, to nurse, to comfort and to cheer."[67]

The slave-owning status of Bishop Polk continues to attract both controversy and uncertainty, as the exact number of slaves he owned has not been the subject of firm agreement. The United States Census of 1840 showed that Polk owned over 100 slaves when in Maury County, Tennessee.[68] Polk's son, William, recorded in his father's biography that upon the transfer of Leighton Plantation to Polk's control, there were "four hundred negroes."[69] The best estimates range from 215 to 400, with the former number recorded by the census of 1850.[70] Regardless of the exact number of slaves owned by Polk at any given point in time, the range of numbers purported by historians of the period undisputedly places him high on the list of clergy who owned slaves in the antebellum South.[71]

There can be no question that religious belief shaped Polk's treatment of his slaves. Even at a time when the sugar plantations of Louisiana worked seven days a week to maximize production, Polk reduced the workweek on his plantation by one day to observe the Sabbath. This was over the objections of his overseers and his neighbors, the latter of whom feared that news would spread that conditions were such at nearby Leighton Plantation.[72] It is a testimony to Polk's steady pastoral influence that apparently his neighbors eventually came to follow his example.[73]

Polk's financial losses multiplied by 1852. This came at a time when, interestingly, his Episcopal and pastoral duties seem to have been both fulfilling and successful. His episcopate in Louisiana witnessed significant growth, from two churches recorded in the state in 1842 to twenty-one churches represented at the diocesan convention in 1853. However, by the following year of 1854, a yellow fever epidemic facilitated the final financial deathblow for Leonidas Polk.[74] Bankruptcy came, and Polk stepped into yet another phase of his life, this one dominated by church planting.

Chapter 4

BISHOP POLK IN
ANTEBELLUM LOUISIANA

"The Ravage of Pestilence"

The story of Leonidas Polk is contained within the broader story of Louisiana, a state carved from the vast territory of the Louisiana Purchase in 1803. The "noble bargain" the United States made with France resulted in Louisiana entering the union as a state on April 30, 1812, the first from the Territory of Orleans. Meeting the population threshold set at sixty thousand residents was rather easy due to the bustling and booming city of New Orleans, but to note the benchmark population of the state does not quite say enough. Anyone who happened to be traveling through the Deep South during the antebellum period would have been struck by the sharp ethno-cultural and socioeconomic diversity of Louisiana, which was a unique mix of Europeans, natives, slaves and free people of color. Antebellum Louisiana was a rich and colorful tapestry of diverse cultures, languages, skin color and religiosity.

The Roman Catholic Church dominated the most populous areas of Louisiana at the middle of the nineteenth century because it had been the state religion of France and therefore all its colonies. Even when France lost the colony of Louisiana at the end of the Seven Years' War with Britain in 1763, the colony passed to Spain, another Roman Catholic country. The area east of the Mississippi River did come under British control, including a vaster territory that encompassed parts of Alabama and Mississippi. The British constructed fortifications near Baton Rouge. However, these developments did little to introduce a diversity of religious populations in the region.

The final years of Spanish control of Louisiana leading up to its transfer back to France by terms of secret treaty in 1798 began to see larger numbers of Anglo-Americans heading west to settle in the region. By the time Louisiana was transferred to the United States, the population was becoming gradually more diverse in its composition.

Because the southern United States primarily represented a settling of white Anglo-Saxon Protestants, the large Roman Catholic population of Louisiana would have struck any observer as a notable oddity as compared to its neighbors. It is a certain fact that counted among the state's diverse population were still large numbers of French-speaking Catholics to provide more than balance for the relatively fewer numbers of Protestants settling there. Louisiana's population during the mid-nineteenth century was also quite scattered, with dense groupings of peoples located near the international port city of New Orleans, yet many rural areas of Louisiana had barely enough population to warrant rigorous counting for the federal census.

Yet every United States census taken from the beginning of the nineteenth century to the eve of the Civil War in 1860 reflected that slaves composed almost half of Louisiana's total population. The institution of slavery was the one constant throughout the Deep South, the economic indicator that bonded Louisiana to its neighbors in a way that transcended any perceived cultural diversity. So dominant were the large sugar cane plantations in Louisiana that one might easily forget the small rural farming establishments that dotted the landscape of the state but were equally significant to the overall prosperity of the region.

A late nineteenth-century history of Louisiana noted with great clarity that "the only things that interrupted the prosperity of the state at this time were Yellow Fever and the overflows of the Mississippi, both of which came with terrible regularity."[75] It is interesting that yellow fever, with its predilection for newcomers with little immunity, may have been responsible for keeping the population of Louisiana Creoles further segregated and ethnically distinct long after assimilation might have been expected.[76] While the social and cultural impact of yellow fever is a matter of ongoing scholarly examination, the certainty was that it was a disease that was a frequent visitor to the state. The "black vomit" arrived with such frightening regularity that the population dreaded the arrival of warm weather each year, never knowing what numbers the final death count might reach.

Yellow fever was cyclical, beginning in the warm months of midsummer and lasting as late as early November when the first true frosts arrived in Louisiana.[77] It was an almost constant feature of life in Louisiana, one that residents seem to have mostly accepted with a grim resolve. The Greater New Orleans area always suffered the worst because of the density of population and continual traffic through its international port. Indeed, the worst epidemic in all of Louisiana occurred in the city of New Orleans in 1853, just one year before it struck at Polk's Leighton Plantation. However, the Great Epidemic of 1853 disobeyed the expected climatic cycle by arriving earlier than the customary midsummer heat. The first death from yellow fever in New Orleans that year was reported in the month of May,[78] surely a harbinger of what was to be a catastrophic epidemic that revisited much of south Louisiana with almost equal fervor the next year.

From Bishop Polk's nearby town of Thibodaux on September 9 was an ominous message from the local postmaster: "Yellow Fever still raging with two hundred sick, seventy deaths up to this morning. Hardly enough of us well to take care of the sick."[79] The small town of Thibodaux lost approximately 10 percent of its total population that year. In a letter to Bishop Stephen Elliott of the Diocese of Georgia in October 1855, Polk observed that the outbreaks of 1854 and 1855 would have been just as bad as that which occurred in New Orleans in 1853 had there been enough people left alive for it affect.[80]

It would be difficult to know which profession was most in demand during times of yellow fever epidemic: physician or clergy. The very high death rates that were at times associated with the disease stressed the ability of either profession to truly respond effectively. The sick and dying called for physician and clergy with equal urgency, and in times of true epidemics, the physician rendered palliative care to the dying and clergy responded with hasty prayers and burials in mass graves. Indeed, records indicate that individual graveside services were not often feasible during severe epidemics due to the sheer numbers of burials to occur on any given day.[81]

The medicine of the nineteenth century was yet crude by current standards, and there appears to have been no standard acknowledged treatment for yellow fever. Physicians across the state all seem to have used their favorite remedies, with regular bleedings and purgings as the most common medical approaches.[82] Not unlike the medieval response to the bubonic plague, the reaction of nineteenth-century science and religion to the pestilence of yellow fever reflected a level of hopeless ignorance. Until the exact cause of yellow fever was identified at the turn of the twentieth century, much of the belief that was expressed in public prayers and in newspaper accounts could only acknowledge a divine cause, as its earthly source remained unknown.

Bishop Polk wrote a prayer that he put in use throughout the Episcopal Diocese of Louisiana to be used in times of epidemic. The prayer asked that God would "turn us from the ravage of the pestilence, wherewith for our inequities, thou are now visiting us."[83] A similar theme was seen in the response of civil authorities as well, including the response of the mayor of New Orleans, who asked during the 1853 epidemic that a day be set aside for "the general voice to rise in supplication to the Almighty God, that He may be pleased to lighten the heavy burden" of the horrific epidemic that summer.[84]

The impact of yellow fever on Louisiana was not only felt in southern areas of the state; indeed, it was a pestilence that knew no favoritism for a certain region. Dr. E.D. Fenner, in a report to the American Medical Association on the extent of the disease in 1854 (the same year that the disease struck Polk's plantation), noted, "It attacked every town along the river, as high as Napoleon, at the mouth of the Arkansas River, every village in Mississippi and Louisiana south of Vicksburg, and almost every plantation along the coast below Natchez."[85] The epidemics had the effect of not only bringing tragedy and loss at a personal level, but they also had adverse economic impacts, as seen in the severe financial blow dealt to Leonidas Polk at Leighton Plantation.

Another important factor during this time in history and of undisputed influence on Leonidas Polk during his episcopacy in Louisiana was the social effect of the Great Awakening. Debate erupted in various intellectual quarters about a rather radical notion that emerged from this unique American religious revival of the eighteenth century—that of Christianizing the slave population. The most important impact of the Great Awakening dealt with the issue of slavery, following a charge led by one of the movement's leaders, George Whitefield, who believed that slaves should receive Christian formation most urgently. Most planters throughout the South naturally feared this, and it produced a divisive class debate framed in theological terms. Whitefield himself observed an economic structure and system in the South that allowed some men to grow wealthy and others to live in complete and desperate poverty. Reacting to this, Whitefield preached about what he had seen as an elite plantation society that was too much of the world and too remotely distant from the teachings of the Christian faith.[86]

While the evangelical zeal of the reforms focused on slavery was quite frightening to much of the landowning class, Leonidas Polk responded to the call of the Great Awakening, as did Bishop Elliott of the Diocese of Georgia.

Bishop Elliott was also instrumental in driving large numbers of slaves into the Episcopal tradition of Christianity and believed quite strongly in the church's mission to the enslaved, despite the reactions of slave owners. The resistance met at the local level to this radical evangelism was explained by a principle deeply rooted in the traditions of the Old South and as old as the American republic itself. The sovereignty of the landowner was a concept so deeply imprinted that it was impossible to fully dislodge it in nineteenth-century society but perhaps most difficult among the plantation owners of the antebellum South. Interestingly, it was a mindset that also made acceptable the enacting of personal reforms, for it meant that while neighboring landowners might disagree with fellow plantation owners, the idea that each owner was sovereign carried the equal weight of that same honor and tradition.[87]

When Polk became bishop of the newly established Diocese of Louisiana in 1842, he had already founded a plantation church for slaves, so he was already known to be a supporter of this aspect of progressive Christian evangelism. This became St. John's Episcopal Church in Thibodaux, still a lively parish at the time of this writing, with the distinction of being the oldest Episcopal church west of the Mississippi River. Bishop Polk supervised the laying of the cornerstone in 1844 and consecrated it on Palm Sunday 1845. A slave gallery was added to the structure for the purpose of

St. John's Episcopal Church, Thibodaux, Louisiana. Bishop Polk established this church in the nearby community of Thibodaux when he owned Leighton Plantation. Polk was greatly influenced by the religious movement known as the Great Awakening, which promoted the radical idea of evangelizing slave populations. St. John's is the oldest Episcopal church west of the Mississippi River, and the building featured a slave gallery. *Courtesy of Michael Pierson, St. John's Episcopal Church, Thibodaux, Louisiana.*

The Polk window at Trinity Episcopal Church in Natchitoches, Louisiana. The stained glass in the bell tower depicts Polk evangelizing a slave. *Photograph by Cheryl White.*

involving local slave populations in the church services,[88] even if segregated from the remainder of the parish. At the time, this represented a radical and undoubtedly unpopular idea, one that helps distinguish Leonidas Polk as an interesting combination of evangelical-progressive in the Protestant Episcopal Church of his day.

Polk's most significant challenge in Christianizing the nearly half of the Louisiana population that was enslaved was directly linked to the fear that many had about the social change likely to result from this extension of Christian education. Bishop Polk had a vision of raising up a specific group within the Diocese of Louisiana that would be charged with the special task of the religious formation of slaves. In 1845, he recommended to the Diocesan Convention that the canons be changed to reflect an order of deacons whose chief function would be slave ministry.[89]

On his own home plantation, the bishop personally celebrated marriage ceremonies for his slaves in a way that reinforced the sacramental nature of the union and spoke volumes about Polk's own beliefs about the need to provide ministry to the enslaved. Polk's daughter recorded:

> *The greatest efforts were made by the bishop to preserve among his servants the sanctity of family life. Their weddings were always celebrated in his home; the broad hall was decorated for the occasion with evergreens and flowers and illuminated with many lights. The bride and groom (all decked in wedding garments presented by Mrs. Polk), with their attendants, were ushered quietly into their master's presence. The honor coveted by the bishop's children, and given as the reward of good behavior, was to hold aloft the silver candlesticks while their father read the marriage service.*[90]

The same account by Polk's daughter hints also at the bishop's policy of forcing the sacrament of marriage on those caught engaged in sexual promiscuity: "If the couple had misbehaved, they were compelled to atone for it by marriage. In that case, there was no display, but the guilty pair were summoned from the field, and in their working clothes, in the study, without flowers or candles, were made husband and wife."[91]

In addition, Polk was reported to have held regular church services on the plantation on the Sundays when he was home, with all expected to be in attendance. As noted previously, Polk's policy of a six-day workweek honoring the Christian Sabbath was unpopular with other plantation owners initially. What seems clear from these accounts is that Polk acutely felt the weight of a personal responsibility to Christianize slaves and was indeed willing to incur the temporary ill will of other Louisiana planters in order to advance this mission work. However, it is an interesting observation that as radical as the notion of slave evangelism was to the antebellum South, neither Polk nor Elliott ever seemed to have believed that the social reforms of this new evangelical ideal extended to freeing slaves.

Leonidas Polk no doubt counted among his evangelical influences that of his own mentor, Charles McIlvaine, who had been instrumental in the establishment of the Protestant Episcopal Society for the Promotion of Evangelical Knowledge (better known by its acronym of PESPEK), founded at the 1847 General Convention. This society grew out of a response to what some Episcopal bishops perceived as a growing threat of the "Tractarians" or "Oxford Movement" that began in 1833 within the Church of England. This movement seemed to want to push Anglicanism back to embrace its Roman roots in both liturgy and doctrine, efforts that made evangelicals nervous. This anxiety had a natural migration to the Protestant Episcopal Church of the United States.[92]

The doctrine of the society that McIlvaine helped found represented all the basic and core ideals of the Reformation with an emphasis on salvation through a conversion experience and a personal relationship with Jesus Christ. The ecclesiology of the society reflected the idea that the church was the invisible body made up of all Christian believers.[93] This differentiation of the evangelical faction took place in such close chronological proximity to Polk's episcopate that he could not have been unaware or unaffected by it. Indeed, he seems to have been a firm adherent to this evangelical response of the Protestant Episcopal Church.

Other events conspired to further shape Bishop Polk's worldview. For much of Polk's episcopacy, he had served with little financial compensation, but this changed following recovery from the yellow fever ravages along Bayou Lafourche in 1854–55. Polk became rector of the newly founded Trinity Episcopal Church in New Orleans, with the understanding that the normal daily operations of the parish would be carried out by an assistant during times when Polk's Episcopal duties required him to be absent.[94] The move to New Orleans was transformative in the life of the Episcopal Church in Louisiana, for Polk's presence in such a large place perhaps contributed to his larger visions. Polk began to further explore a dream he later claimed he had for a while—that of establishing a great university. As Polk's wife later recalled after her husband's death, "In the spring of 1852 he [Polk] began to collect information relative to the educational system of England, France and Prussia, and to consult with some of his friends on the feasibility of founding a University of the South."[95]

Although Polk's son and first biographer stated his father had long held the idea of a southern university as an ideal that he hoped one day to be part of, it was Polk's experience as a missionary bishop that doubtlessly helped to drive the idea forward. In that capacity, Polk had been acutely aware of the lack of trained clergy and experienced this throughout large portions of the South. At this time also came his decision to sell Leighton Plantation. Was this because of financial burdens, as observed by many biographers, or was it because it became increasingly difficult for Polk to reconcile the wealth of a sugar planter with the duties of a priest and bishop? Did the influence of the Great Awakening and the evangelism of George Whitefield shape him also in this way? As with each phase of his life, the ending of the Leighton Plantation chapter opened a new one, as Polk turned to the idea of the University of the South.

Polk's vision for this university seems to have not only been about raising up educated laity and training clergy to fill a void in the Protestant Episcopal Church; it seems to have also been about a deep pride he felt in the unique culture of the South. In 1856, he urged the bishops of nine dioceses in the South to help build this university in Tennessee. In response, the dioceses sent representatives in 1857 to a planning meeting held on Lookout Mountain. The rest is a matter of record attested to by the edifices of University of the South today. Polk laid the cornerstone in 1860, by which time the very name of the school evoked emotional reactions in the raging sectional controversies that were to imminently erupt in a bloody civil war.[96]

Bishop James Hervey Otey of Tennessee denied that the University of the South was to be an exclusively southern university in an effort to dispel the immediate reactions from fellow bishops in the North. Otey stated in his memoirs that the University of the South was designed to be "an institution of conservatism," and he saw the school as a means of actually quelling the controversy by "binding the discordant elements into a Union stronger than steel."[97] Polk's legacy continues to be profoundly felt there today, where it still provides seminary training for Episcopal clergy.

James Hervey Otey, the Episcopal bishop of the Diocese of Tennessee. When Polk left the Diocese of Louisiana to serve in the Confederate command structure, Otey volunteered to make Episcopal visits to Louisiana to cover Polk's duties as necessary. However, Otey's poor health prohibited him from ever doing this.

Throughout the Louisiana he traveled, Polk planted church communities that bear his imprint yet today. It is hard to visit any community in the state with an Episcopal church and not hear of him; the

Episcopal culture of the state reverberates still with the very mention of his name. From the banks of Bayou Lafourche to the banks of the Red River in Shreveport, his church-planting legacy is visible. In Shreveport, the annals of city history claim the first church service ever held on the banks of the Red River in what would become that port city was led by Leonidas Polk. In that year of 1839, Shreveport was only a fledgling frontier city on a river struggling to be a major inland waterway and serve as a gateway to the West. According to numerous histories of Shreveport, the first Episcopal congregation gathered in an unfinished building near the river while Polk celebrated the Eucharist over the noise of raucous dockworkers not far away. Polk's story is nothing if not replete with colorful anecdotes such as this one that characterize the entire period of his Episcopal tenure.

Church growth during Polk's time as bishop of Louisiana was steady and sure. The records of the 1853 General Convention of the Protestant Episcopal Church show that there were twenty-one clergy canonically resident in the Diocese of Louisiana that year.[98] By the time General Convention met in 1859, just six years later, the record reflected over 50 percent growth in canonically resident clergy to thirty-three.[99] It was a time in the history of the Protestant Episcopal Church that also saw the introduction of controversy over the publication of essays and reviews by seven Church of England clergy. The essays appeared shortly after the publication of Charles Darwin's work *On the Origin of the Species* and collectively challenged a traditionalist approach to biblical criticism. The House of Bishops denounced the works in 1860,[100] but the Anglican presence in North America seems to have been relatively unaffected by the intellectual controversy. However, the same cannot be said for Louisiana and the looming political controversies of the era.

By the decade of the 1850s in Louisiana, as well as in other states across the Deep South, there was indeed a growing sectionalism resonating from virtually every quarter. The road to the Civil War was in fact a long one in American history, with notable political efforts and manipulations throughout the nineteenth century to prolong its course, but the 1850s witnessed some of the most brutal sectional violence to date. In May 1854, Congress finalized the Kansas-Nebraska Act, culminating in a violent series of events known collectively as "Bleeding Kansas." Two years later, on the floor of the United States Congress, the violence became individualized as Representative Preston Brooks from South Carolina physically assaulted Senator Charles Sumner from Massachusetts. The sectionalism that drove both incidences of violence was by then pervasive in the American republic.[101] Meanwhile,

Bishop Polk in Antebellum Louisiana

John Brown's raid on Harpers Ferry in 1859 solidified the proslavery stance of those in the South committed to maintaining the status quo.

In many ways, reactions in Louisiana to these events on the national stage predictably mirrored those of neighboring southern states yet were always tempered by the special conditions that existed within its own borders. The Louisiana congressional delegation supported the Kansas-Nebraska Act, which called for the issue of slavery to be settled by "popular sovereignty" of the settlers. John Brown's raid was loudly denounced throughout Louisiana as frightening and fanatical. Still, the vote for the state's secession from the Union, when it came in 1861, was far from unanimous. It can be said that Louisiana itself was beset by its own unique sectionalism, probably born of the same cultural diversity that had always set it somewhat apart from its southern neighbors. The road to secession in Louisiana ultimately led to the Confederate States of America, where the story of Leonidas Polk took yet another unpredictable turn.

Chapter 5

LOUISIANA SECESSION POLITICS, WAR AND THE PROTESTANT EPISCOPAL CHURCH

"A Man Whose House Is on Fire"

D uring the years 1860–61, Bishop Polk carried out his Episcopal duties for the Diocese of Louisiana in a manner that belied any foreboding he might have had about presidential politics, the road to Louisiana secession or its possible aftermath. In addition to rigorously supervising the ongoing construction at University of the South, Polk's ministry was busy with his characteristic energy and enthusiasm. The record shows that in that final year before the outbreak of the Civil War, he oversaw the building of five new churches in the diocese and a reorganization of a parish in Bastrop and witnessed the admission of those new parishes at the annual Diocesan Convention in May 1861.[102] However, the record also reveals that he was at least partially preoccupied and concerned with the developing events that would ultimately erupt in war.

The secession of many southern states seemed imminent following the presidential election of November 1860, and Polk would have been able to critically read the political landscape of Louisiana, for he knew its people well. Amidst all the discussion of secession politics that year, clergy throughout the South seemed reluctant to support such an idea, but this was especially true perhaps for clergy in the Protestant Episcopal Church. The bishop of Alabama, Nicholas Cobbs, prophetically said he would rather die than see the state leave the Federal Union. Interestingly, he died the very same day that Alabama withdrew from the United States.[103] Bishop Otey of Tennessee was quite outspoken against secession and purposefully seems to have avoided the use of separatist rhetoric in his diocesan communications. Furthermore, Otey, unlike Bishop Polk, did not authorize any changes to the public prayers section of the Book of Common Prayer in use in his diocese.[104]

Bishop Polk wrote to President James Buchanan on December 26, 1860, just two days after South Carolina issued its *Declaration of Immediate Causes Which Induce and Justify the Secession of South Carolina from the Federal Union*. This letter was both informative and eerily prophetic:

> *My position and opportunities give me the amplest facilities for knowing the actual State of mind of the people of Louisiana and of the surrounding Southern states, and I write to say that I am thoroughly convinced that they have deliberately and inflexibly resolved to cut themselves off from the Union. This feeling is deepening and widening every day, and no difference exists except the mode of effecting it. To attempt to prevent it by force of arms would instantly extinguish that difference and unite the whole population as one man…But whatever the determination of national executive may be, they have resolved to accept that determination, to plant themselves on what they hold to be their rights, and to resist all efforts to infringe them.*

Polk went on to instruct Buchanan just as a prophet might speak: "I have not a doubt that Georgia, Florida, Alabama, Mississippi and Louisiana will all have followed the example of South Carolina, and will be out of the union by the first of February; that they will have formed a separate government by the first of March; and that other southern states will sooner or later all join them."[105] Polk seems to have indeed had a firm grasp on the events as they were developing and predicted with clarity the outcome of the coming months of Louisiana and United States history.

It is still subject of considerable debate among historians and scholars of Louisiana the exact nature of public opinion on the eve of the state's decision to leave the Union. Did the vote of the delegates meeting in special convention in January 1861 truly represent the general will of the people? There was certainly a strong anti-secession sentiment in and around the international port city of New Orleans, with so much of the area's economic vitality linked to an ongoing relationship with the United States. However, the actions of state officials indicated a predictable outcome, and many who opposed secession may have felt threatened into remaining silent.[106]

While it may not have been a unanimous decision for Louisiana to secede from the union, it was also not a sudden or unexpected one. Louisiana, like the rest of the South, came to this process through a period of protracted unrest, culminating in the November 1860 election of Abraham Lincoln—a man who had not even appeared on the presidential ballot in Louisiana. The governor, Thomas Overton Moore, set the tone for secession shortly after his election in January 1860 by making divisive public statements about what the recent national election had proved to the people of Louisiana—that there was a certain northern intent to destroy the rights of slaveholders.[107]

Months before Louisiana seceded from the Union there were harbingers of separation. Louisiana's delegates to the national Democratic Party convention that year were among the wealthiest planters in the state. The meeting convened on April 21, 1860, in Charleston, South Carolina, but less than ten days later, Louisiana had separated itself from the rank and file of the national party. This was due to dissatisfaction with the notion of "popular sovereignty" as a plank in the party platform.[108] The very idea that a state's population would be left to decide the issue of slavery within its own territory was threatening to southern slaveholders, for this freedom of expression left room for the balance of power to be tipped against the South.

When Louisianans went to the polls to cast votes for president on November 6, the tally spoke clearly. John C. Breckinridge, a staunch defender of states' rights, carried the state of Louisiana with 22,681 votes. John Bell registered a close second with a total of 20,204 votes, and Stephen A. Douglas, the "popular sovereignty" Democrat, netted only 7,625 votes.[109] The winner of the White House, Abraham Lincoln, got not a single Louisiana vote due to being omitted from the ballot.

Naturally, Louisiana reacted harshly to the news of Lincoln's election. Almost immediately, military preparations began with the mobilization of the "Minute Men" of Louisiana. Also, Governor Moore called for a special session of the Louisiana legislature to meet in December of that year, a gathering in which he spoke directly about secession as the only natural and logical course of action. There was a sense of division within division, however, for the "secession fever" in Louisiana took one of two separate identifiable forms as calls went up for a special convention to be held early in 1861. One was either a "secessionist," who favored immediate departure from the Federal Union, or one was a "cooperationist," who favored waiting to consult with other southern states in order to act in concert and therefore with stronger impact. The manifestation of this division took shape on the convention floor on January 26 with a vote of 113–17 for the immediate secession of Louisiana, with some cooperationists wanting to hold off the secession action until later or perhaps avoid it altogether.

Even before the special convention could meet to vote on the weighty issue at hand, Governor Moore seemed to believe it was already a foregone conclusion. On January 9, 1861, nearly three weeks before secession, he ordered troops from New Orleans to go to Baton Rouge, the state capital, to seize the Federal arsenal there. On January 10, state militia traveled south from New Orleans to Forts St. Philip and Jackson, demanding the surrender of those Federal outposts. These garrisons promptly surrendered without putting up a fight, and they became the key defenses of the city of New Orleans during the Union occupation. It is obviously true that even before the official vote for secession was taken among the state's elected delegation, Louisiana had committed itself to an irrevocable course of action.[110] How much the convention's vote to secede was influenced by these gubernatorial actions can be anyone's guess.

There seems to be no question that Leonidas Polk was in full sympathy with the secession cause. Due to his training at West Point Academy, he saw his duty as citizen first to the state of Louisiana and only secondarily to the federal government.[111] However, what of the role of the Protestant Episcopal Church, a national body, within a state that had seceded from the Federal Union? Polk saw the church inextricably bound to this issue of separation in a way that left little room for debate or dispute. Furthermore, he was able to frame his doctrine of separation for both the diocesan church and the state of Louisiana during the crisis in a completely seamless and complementary manner.

On December 28, 1860, in the wake of South Carolina's secession, President Buchanan called for a national day of prayer and reflection. Polk wrote to his diocesan clergy in a pastoral letter asking them to observe the president's request and provided for them the following prayer specifically for this use: "O Almighty God, the Fountain of all wisdom and the Helper of all who call upon thee, we thy unworthy servants, under a deep sense of the difficulties and dangers by which we are now surrounded, turn ourselves to thee in earnest supplication and prayer."[112]

Polk's prophecy with regard to Louisiana secession proved startlingly accurate. On January 26, 1861, the state passed an ordinance of secession and withdrew from the United States. Just four days later, Polk issued yet another pastoral letter to the diocese:

> The State of Louisiana, having, by a formal ordinance, through her delegates in convention assembled, withdrawn herself from all further

connection with the United States of America, and constituted herself a
separate sovereignty, has, by that act, removed our diocese from the pale
of "The Protestant Episcopal Church in the United States." We have,
therefore, an independent diocesan existence.[113]

As for the relationship of the Diocese of Louisiana to the remainder of
the national church, Polk went further to frame his understanding of church
unity in the same terms by which he understood secular unity:

With us, it is a separation, not division; certainly not alienation. And there
is no reason why, if we should find the union of our dioceses under one
national Church impracticeable, we should cease to feel for each other the
respect and regard with which purity of manners, high principle, and a
manly devotion to truth never fail to inspire generous minds. Our relations
to each other hereafter will be the relations we both now hold to the men of
our mother-church of England.[114]

Also true to prophecy was the fact that the new Confederate States
of America was constituted before Polk's predicted date of March 1,
given in his previous letter to President Buchanan. In response to that
development, Polk further instructed the clergy of the Diocese of
Louisiana to make appropriate substitutions in the public prayers for
civil authorities.[115]

Polk's choice of the word "independent" to describe the diocese was
perhaps an unfortunate one; certainly it was one that initiated unease
among his colleagues in the House of Bishops. Although Polk clearly used
the term to reflect his understanding that the diocese was located within the
geographic borders of a state and therefore could not remain tethered to
the national Protestant Episcopal Church, his terminology elicited anxiety
throughout the church. Bishop Otey of Tennessee urged Polk to remember
he was bound by his consecration oath to "the discipline and worship of the
Protestant Episcopal Church."[116]

In response, Polk attempted to lend clarity to his position through
differentiating the church in a secular environment from the invisible union
of all Christians. In a March 28, 1861 pastoral letter, he explained that a
change in church *union* did not necessarily indicate a change in *unity.* Polk
remained Anglican in his perspective and saw the Diocese of Louisiana as
remaining invisibly but historically identified with the Protestant Episcopal
Church through those same Anglican roots.

Throughout this anxious time, Bishop Polk's correspondence underscored his attempts to continue to read and report the progress of separation and the looming war, yet in the process, he also gives remarkable glimpses of ordinary life during this time in Louisiana history. In a letter he penned to his wife from New Orleans on April 26, 1861, he wrote:

> *My beloved wife: I am now at the stock landing, on the steamer* Hodge, *which is putting out cattle. I found, on my return to Shreveport, that I could not get to my appointment in Minden because of a change in the schedule in the stages, and so I had to give it up. I came, therefore, to New Orleans in this boat…the whole world is in arms, in the country and in the town. All are agreed now. There are not two parties anymore.*[117]

By the time Polk wrote this letter in late April, it was obvious that the southern secession was not going to pass into history as a peaceful event. With hostilities exchanged at Fort Sumter, South Carolina, on April 12–13, war already seemed inevitable to most observers. Polk naturally reverted to both his upbringing in the Polk family and his military training, becoming a soldier again. He assumed because of his training at West Point that war would be a fair fight among honorable men, all uniformed combatants acting with rules of engagement under the flags of their separate nations. Not until he learned of the burning of the home near Sewanee into which he had recently settled his wife did it occur to him that this war might be otherwise.[118]

Polk was also hopeful that the church would be able to play a significant role in stemming the violence and quelling the passions for war to spill over into the civilian populations. He constantly looked to the church as a beacon of hope. This perspective led him to consider the affairs in the Diocese of Louisiana. He and his friend Bishop Elliott of Georgia had hoped to call together a new "national" meeting of southern Episcopalians, but this idea met with some initial reluctance on behalf of his Louisiana clergy. However, this proved to be the overriding theme of the 1861 diocesan convention, and the topic could not be avoided.

It is notable that Polk continued to use the term "diocesan independence" even after criticism from the broader church. In his convention address of 1861, Polk emphasized the term again when he said, "The normal condition of the diocese of the Catholic Church is that of *separate independence* and a departure from that condition has ever been the fruit of expediency only."[119] Polk appealed to Christian history to lend legitimacy to his argument that

Stephen Elliott, Episcopal bishop of Georgia and friend of Bishop Polk. Elliott supported Polk's decision to join the Confederate army and, like Polk, had been profoundly impacted by the theology of the Great Awakening and supported the evangelization of slaves. Elliott also gave the elegy at Polk's funeral in 1864. *Courtesy of Diocese of Georgia.*

the severing of ties with the United States created no crisis for the Episcopal Church due to its diocesan structure. Indeed, Polk relied on history to argue that dioceses constituted themselves together when the Protestant Episcopal Church was formed; therefore, the diocese preceded the national church.

Polk's address to the diocesan convention that year expanded this historical approach:

> *There was a time in the history of the church in Louisiana when it was not under the authority of the constitution of the Protestant Episcopal Church in the United States of America, and when there was no constitutional union existing between it and the dioceses in the United States...in accepting the constitution connection...our diocese did not intend to impose upon herself impossible obligations which in any future contingency would conflict with her duties to Christ...while the Church is entirely free from interference on the part of the State, she is nevertheless not exempt from the consequences and action of the State.*[120]

A special committee of that convention composed of both orders (lay and clergy) was to report an opinion and, after study, returned a report that affirmed Bishop Polk's position. However, the committee drafted a resolution that was careful to avoid the term "diocesan independence." As a result, the resolution that came forward for consideration met with no substantial opposition. Reverend Dr. Charles Goodrich, rector of St. Paul's in New Orleans, previously had been vocal in his opposition to Polk's position. He was reluctant to believe that an instrument of secession from the Federal Union could by any manner or means initiate a separation from the national Protestant Episcopal Church. Yet even Dr. Goodrich became reconciled to the position of his bishop and the special committee appointed for its study. In convention, he rose only to say that it appeared to him that the separation of the diocese from the national church had been effected by the instrument of secession and he would not speak against the diocesan resolution:[121]

> *RESOLVED that The Diocese of Louisiana, loyal to the doctrine, discipline and example of the holy Catholic Church, and closely following the model of our mother Church of England and our sister dioceses in the United States, is desirous of entering into union with the remaining dioceses of the Confederate states for the formation of a national Protestant Episcopal Church in the Confederate States of America.*[122]

It is interesting to note that Polk's understanding of the diocese as historically "independent" did not in any measure deter him from immediately seeking another union to be constituted with other southern dioceses in an alternative "national" structure. Clearly, the model of a national identity for the diocese was an idea that had considerable merit in Polk's view.

While the action of Louisiana and other southern Episcopal dioceses might be the subject of debate, the calling of a meeting of southern deputies from the now-separated dioceses might not have been possible without the work of Bishops Polk and Elliott. It is also fair to say that there might have been other consequences resulting had other southern dioceses not been encouraged to meet, discuss and remain together until after the war. Likely, the constituting of southern dioceses was precisely what made possible the reconciliation of the Protestant Episcopal Church after the war. Polk believed that without a breach of unity or affection, the provincial union of northern and southern dioceses had ceased to exist. It was a credit to his evangelical background that he was able to articulate this invisible unity as he understood it, and therefore he saw no cessation to the complete unity of the Protestant Episcopal Church and, indeed, the Anglican communion around the world.

In retrospect, the historian might be tempted to judge the actions of Bishop Polk in this regard. However, had the Confederacy won the war and therefore established a separate nation in North America, there would be no question but that another province of Anglicanism would have been the foregone outcome. The seceded states did not enter war with a plan for failure nor with an eye to reconciling with the Federal Union. Therefore, Polk did not envision a return to the national Protestant Episcopal Church as it then existed. In the absence of something, there was nothing, and Polk obviously planned for another eventual entity to exist in the new Confederate States of America.

From this point forward, Polk seemed to have turned his attention to becoming a soldier again. In early May 1861, he wrote to Confederate president Jefferson Davis to express his concerns about what he thought to be an imminent Union invasion of the South. In his response, Davis invited Polk to come to Richmond to consult and further share his concerns.[123] At that Richmond gathering, Davis offered Polk a command in the Confederate army, seemingly more urgent at the time because of the present lack of availability of Albert Sidney Johnston to serve.[124] Therefore, Davis offered Polk the rank of major general, whereupon Polk's initial response was to decline.

In a letter to Bishop Elliott, Polk reflected on the Richmond meeting and Davis's offer: "The matter has been before me for a week. I have consulted some judicious friends in and out of the Church, among them old Father

President Jefferson Davis of the Confederate States of America. A friend of Leonidas Polk since their days at West Point Military Academy, Davis relied on Polk's friendship more than his military acumen. By the end of the war, the lack of communication within the Confederate government and military command structure was an obvious liability. *Courtesy of Library of Congress, Civil War Prints and Photographs Division, Washington, D.C.*

Albert Sidney Johnston, Polk's West Point roommate and friend. Johnston's army deployment on the Pacific coast delayed his availability for Confederate service when war broke out in 1861, and his absence figured decisively in Polk's decision to take the commission as major general. Johnston was killed in action at the Battle of Shiloh in 1862. *Courtesy of Library of Congress, Civil War Prints and Photographs Division, Washington, D.C.*

Meade."[125] Polk spoke about the matter of his diocesan responsibilities, which weighed heavily on his mind at this time, but also revealed an understanding of the superiority of the duty to which he was now called: "As to my diocese, I have, of course, not had time to consult it, nor would I have done so if I had. This is such a case as I should, I think, decide for myself. I shall not resign my charge of it, but shall write them that I have undertaken this work because it seemed the duty next."[126]

Whether Polk's decision was rooted in his familial link to the Patriots of the American Revolution, his conviction of the correctness of the Southern cause or both is a matter for speculation. His initial reluctance at accepting Jefferson Davis's offer seems to indicate he was not easily persuaded to take up the sword. However, there can be no question that once the decision was made, the ease with which Polk made the transition to the battlefield was somewhat unsettling for many in Louisiana. Even in the secessionist South, the appropriate role for clergy, even those who had trained in military academies during their youth, was not to take up arms but to mount the pulpit and provide divine sustenance for the military cause.

However, not everyone shared the understanding that clergy had no place on the fields of war. An interesting anecdote illustrates this, involving a young Louisiana woman named Sarah Dorsey, whom Polk had confirmed in 1857. Dorsey made a general's banner for Polk, modeled on the shields carried by Roman soldiers during the time of Emperor Constantine the Great. In a letter from Dorsey to Polk, she wrote, "We are fighting the Battle of the Cross against modern Barbarians."[127]

Among his fellow bishops, Polk found affection and support. In November 1861, Bishop Otey of Tennessee visited Polk in Union City, Kentucky, and recorded his impressions in his personal diary: "He stands higher in my love and esteem than ever."[128] Otey also promised Polk he would make visitations to the Diocese of Louisiana, but Otey's failing health made it impossible for him to do so.[129]

In an often-repeated anecdote, Bishop-General Polk, when asked why he would throw off the bishop's gown for the sword of a general, responded, "I buckle the sword over the gown."[130] This iconic statement, ever attributed to Polk, does in fact sum up his attitude toward the battlefield. Citing the command offer from Jefferson Davis as "a Call of Providence," Polk couched his justification for taking up arms in obedience to a summons from God. Yet for Polk, there was always the plan of resuming his apostolic ministry. He even said a few days before his death in Georgia that he felt as "a man whose house is on fire, and who has left his business to put it out. As soon as the war is over I shall return to my proper calling."[131]

Chapter 6

MAJOR GENERAL LEONIDAS POLK IN THE MISSISSIPPI VALLEY, 1861

"That the Lord Will Deliver Us Out of Their Hands"

H istorians of the American Civil War have done exhaustive examinations of Polk's military service, and it is not within the scope of this work to either repeat or revise this aspect of Polk's life. To be sure, it is covered in considerable detail in the countless works that survey the actions in the western theater of the war, many of which are harshly critical of Polk, particularly with regard to matters in Kentucky in 1861. Transitioning from bishop to general was more challenging than Polk himself seems to have believed, and many a contemporary observer believed the rank of general to be above Polk's merit and experience. Historians have even gone as far as to suggest that the blame for the Confederate loss of the war can rest squarely on Polk's shoulders for his invasion of Kentucky, while others have argued that perhaps his failure was in not acting quickly enough.[132]

Polk received his commission as major general on June 25, 1861, and on July 4, he received his assignment to Department No. 2, headquartered in Memphis, Tennessee. This was a department of the provisional army of the Confederacy that encompassed the Mississippi River Valley, including western Tennessee, eastern Arkansas, Louisiana north of the Red River, parts of northern Mississippi and Alabama—chiefly, those areas that either bordered on or were strategically important to the Mississippi River. This part of the South was a transportation center, with a complex network of

A fortification on the Tennessee River, western theater, circa 1861–65. The Union objective in the western theater was to cut key Confederate rail lines and supply centers. Control of the Mississippi and Tennessee Rivers was crucial to a Union victory. *Courtesy of Library of Congress, Civil War Prints and Photographs Division, Washington, D.C.*

rail, steamboats and other transport vessels that worked the Mississippi River. The region of Polk's command was not only the economic hub of the new Confederate States of America but was also vitally central to the Union objective of a decisive and speedy outcome to the conflict.

Polk was welcomed with all the pomp and enthusiasm of a Roman triumph as he arrived in Memphis that summer, but the remainder of his days in the Confederate service would be marked by controversy.[133] Polk's appearance prompted a popular reaction among the people of Tennessee that they had "the sword of the Lord [Polk] and of Gideon [General Gideon Pillow]" as a means of defense.[134] As the commander of Department No.

2, Polk was immediately thrust into the role of responsibility for the most important defensive maneuvering of the war—that of the Mississippi River. That Polk understood the significance of the task to which he had been charged is not in question, but his anxiety about the vulnerability of the Confederate position may have caused him to act in haste.

One can read a measure of insecurity in Polk's reluctance to take the command in the first place. Although he felt honored by Jefferson Davis's confidence in him, he nevertheless believed the command should have gone to Albert Sidney Johnston or Robert E. Lee and asked Davis to alter his command orders. Johnston was not yet available, and Lee was needed in Virginia. Since everyone feared an imminent invasion of the Confederate capital at Richmond, the supporting commands of Joseph Johnston and P.G.T. Beauregard were also thought to be more critical in that region.[135]

Polk acquiesced and took the command of Department No. 2 on July 13 with the understanding that he would relinquish it as soon as Albert Sidney Johnston could arrive. Polk assumed the charge of equipping and training approximately twenty-two thousand men in the newly formed Army of Tennessee. In addition, he was to undertake the development of a border state policy for Missouri and Kentucky.[136] Either of these charges would have been challenging to any army officer of recent experience and repute, but into this job stepped Leonidas Polk, most recently bishop of the Episcopal Diocese of Louisiana and over thirty years removed from West Point Academy.

Fairness requires acknowledging the contradictory nature of two of Polk's assigned objectives, for his actions in one aspect would inevitably leave him vulnerable in the other. To have been simultaneously tasked with observing the declared neutrality of the border states of Missouri and Kentucky and with securing defenses on the Mississippi River was to be poised for failure in one of these endeavors. The success of the river defense initiative clearly negated the ability to maintain a posture of neutrality in Federal states that bordered the Mississippi River.

Not much can be known about Polk's thoughts regarding the enormity of his task, but his actions are known. He acted in a way that clearly indicated he understood the river defenses to be his primary directive. While on his way to Memphis from Richmond, Polk passed through eastern Tennessee and noted that many of the people were in sympathy with the Union; he also noted with unease the proximity of major rail lines passing through this territory. Polk thought it wise to convene a meeting of those from the western and eastern parts of the state to discuss the tense situation. A letter from Polk to this chosen deputation strikes at the heart of one of his greatest strengths, which was to draw upon principles of conciliation: "I am satisfied that many of our fellow countrymen in East Tennessee have, by the course of events, been forced into occupying a position in regard to the question pending between the North and the South which is hardly in keeping with their natural relations, and from which it is our duty, in a spirit of magnanimity, to do what we can to relieve them."[137]

Therefore, one of his first acts was to contact Tennessee governor Harris and dispatch militia into the eastern corner of the state. At this early point, none of the Tennessee state militia had yet been integrated into the Confederate army. To this task, Polk set General Felix Zollicoffer, a former journalist from Tennessee. In spite of a lack of military experience, Zollicoffer's political associations earned him the rank of brigadier general upon his volunteering for service in 1861.[138] Polk's advice to Zollicoffer about how to deal with Tennesseans with Unionist tendencies was to the point and continued to draw upon principles of genteel treatment and unity:

> *I feel confident that, if they are assured by their southern fellow countrymen of their disposition to treat them with kindness, and to respect their manly feelings, while they are making provision for the protection of our own Tennessee soil against invasion from the North, they will have no reason to feel aggrieved by the presence of troops in their midst. They must see that the policy of the United States Government is to overrun and subjugate us…advise them to waive their opposition to the decision of the majority of voters of the state, and to become hereafter, as heretofore, with us a united band of brothers.*[139]

It is important to point out that both Missouri and Kentucky had adopted an official policy of neutrality, which meant that the states were not to be entered unless some action on the part of the United States made such a maneuver necessary. This was a grand ideal that would prove impossible. Both states had divided populations, some of whom had favored and agitated for secession and were therefore willing, covertly if necessary, to provide aid and comfort to the Confederates. However, both states also had large populations of staunch Unionists who worked against such efforts. In many ways, border states represented a microcosm of the state of affairs between the United and Confederate States of America. Some in the border states even advocated for "armed neutrality," which would discourage both Federal and Confederate troops, but even President Lincoln recognized the impossibility of such. In his Congressional address of July 4, 1861, Lincoln noted, "Under the guise of neutrality, it would tie the hands of the Union men and freely pass supplies from among them to the insurrectionists, which it could not do as an open enemy."[140]

For Union efforts in the region, and with the same prime objective of securing the Mississippi River, Lincoln created the Department of the West, which stretched from Illinois to the Rocky Mountains. Major General John C. Fremont was Polk's counterpart in the United States, with orders from Lincoln to push down the Mississippi River toward Memphis, a policy that of course involved the bordering city of St. Louis in Missouri. It was impossible for Missouri to remain out of the line of fire, especially in a state that had already suffered much bloodshed in the violent sectionalism of the 1850s.[141] Fremont learned quickly that this was the case, and he crossed the line of military command by making presidential policy, causing him to run afoul of his commander in chief almost immediately.[142]

Polk read the developing situation in Missouri as imminently threatening, with the arrival of Union troops making obvious the need to respond. Although the official policy of the Confederate government was also not to interfere in border states, Polk was a man of action who read this as an aggressive act in a neutral territory, and he was able to observe firsthand the looming threat. Polk wrote to Confederate secretary of war LeRoy Pope Walker on July 21, just a week after he assumed command, expressing a desire to make decisions contrary to stated policy:

> *The Governor of Tennessee is still waiting for the information he has been soliciting, as I understand him, from the War Department as to certain details, before he transfers his army. In the meantime, he consents that I allow that army to be directed by me in certain operations I now deem expedient in Missouri. I have therefore directed General Pillow to detach from a force in the western district of Tennessee a column of 6000 troops of various arms, and to make a movement on Missouri through New Madrid. He will be joined, as soon as he lands, by 3000 Missourians, now posted near that place, and as he goes forward, by other forces that are prepared to come to him.*[143]

By July 18, General Pillow had in fact occupied New Madrid, on the Mississippi River in Missouri, just forty-two miles southwest of the greater objective of Cairo, Illinois. However, within days Polk realized the deficiency of the troops and the questionable sustainability of their position. They were poorly equipped and their numbers far less than Polk had been led to believe. Also, he had no further men under his command with whom to reinforce New Madrid.

Polk hastily penned another letter to Walker: "This abatement of the force disposable for the invasion of Missouri has caused me to pause in the execution of the plan indicated. I shall proceed to fortify my position at New Madrid with a view of making it a base of operations, and will move forward as soon as circumstances may allow."[144]

Polk's use of terminology in correspondence—the "invasion of Missouri"—indicates with clarity his view that the conditions within the border state justified violating the policy of neutrality. Meanwhile, General Hardee and a force of approximately three thousand men moved to Greenville in Missouri, indicating a readiness to cooperate with the efforts of General Pillow in securing the state. Polk ordered Pillow to abandon New Madrid and join with Hardee's force. Hardee and Pillow had difficulty in communicating and coordinating their joint efforts. Pillow urged a course of action directed at Cape Girardeau as a base for movement on St. Louis; Hardee insisted on an alternative course.

By the end of August 1861, the plan that Polk had for Missouri had come to an end, in spite of successful action at Wilson's Creek on August 10. The forces in Missouri were afterward in no position to proceed; Polk had no confidence in the numbers and encountered among Missourians an unwillingness to be recruited into the cause.[145] He wrote to Jefferson Davis at the end of the month explaining the failure in Missouri and asking to be relieved of this particular command duty. Was Polk aware of his shortcomings? Did he truly believe himself inferior to Albert Sidney Johnston? Or had he felt the tug of his original ministry calling and yearned to return to his diocese in Louisiana?

For these operations to be directed wisely, harmoniously, and successfully, they should be combined from west to east across the Mississippi valley, and placed under the direction of one head. Such a position is one of great responsibility, involving and requiring large experience and extensive military knowledge, and I know of no one so well equal to the task as our friend General Albert Sidney Johnston...I am informed that our friend General Johnston is daily expected. I beg respectfully, but earnestly, to urge upon you the expediency of this appointment. The success of our campaign in this valley may depend upon such an arrangement, and I know of no man who has the capacity to fill the position, who could be had, but General Johnston.[146]

Jefferson Davis responded from Richmond just a few days later. Accompanying the missive were new orders making it clear that Polk was not presently to be replaced but, indeed, was to have his command expanded to include Arkansas, a move that Davis believed would make Polk's original Missouri design more tactically feasible. By now, Polk was convinced that the opportunity in Missouri had passed, so he wanted to turn his full attention to the defenses of the river.[147] Davis wrote his reply in a way that reveals the great affection and friendship between the two men, something that proved to be a liability for the Confederate military command structure but also reveals that in these early days of the conflict, Davis understood the challenges they faced:

> *I regret to learn that you find an unwillingness to volunteer for the war. You know the disadvantage of the constant repetition of the scenes of sickness and sorrow attendant upon the encampments of raw troops. The efficiency of the seasoned and instructed troops can alone ensure success to our army. The enemy are profiting by their first lessons. Would that our people would learn from their example...Keep me better advised of your forces and purposes. It is only when forewarned that I can meet your wishes or your wants. In proportion as our means are small, so do we need to have long notice...May God have you in his keeping, and bless your efforts with all deserved success. Sincerely, your friend, Jefferson Davis.*[148]

Kentucky, also a border state with a divided population, was in many ways more volatile and vulnerable than Missouri. Polk was rightly skeptical that Kentucky would be able to keep Federal troops out. He saw the first line of defense northward on the Mississippi River at Columbus, Kentucky; secondarily, he kept a watchful eye also on Paducah.[149] Meanwhile, President Lincoln had adopted a moderate policy of watchful waiting with regard to Kentucky. Although he never recognized that Kentucky had a right to neutrality, after events in Missouri Lincoln likely saw a need to moderate Federal action. Leaders in Kentucky feared each side for different reasons, and each side viewed Kentucky through the lens necessitated by its objectives. Kentucky feared an "invasion" by either side but knew that a Union occupation could drive some of the state's population to the Confederate cause. Likewise, the Confederate policy toward state neutrality was inhibited by a self-expressed doctrine framed on states' rights. To invade a state with proclaimed neutrality was to violate that doctrine of states' rights in an obvious and contradictory manner.

Lincoln knew the problem with recognizing "neutrality" of a Federal state is that the logic required to do so actually supports the claim of secessionists—that a state can make sovereign decisions related to its relationship with the Federal Union. Recognizing neutrality in this instance would allow a state to reject a lawful directive of the Federal government, therefore implying that the state had the constitutional legitimacy to do so. However, Lincoln also knew that if Kentucky did not suffer any violence in its borders as Missouri had, then a Unionist loyalty might be able to take firmer hold, enough so that it would desire to lose its stated "neutrality" and, in fact, enter the war effort voluntarily for the United States. More than anything else, Polk has been criticized for moving aggressively and hastily into Kentucky, thereby making Lincoln's vision a reality.

The governor of Kentucky, Beriah Magoffin, wrote Jefferson Davis asking the same respectful posture from the Confederacy, to which Davis agreed, but only if the events within Kentucky proved to the Confederacy that the state was, in fact, truly neutral.[150] Yet even as Davis was apparently trying to conciliate and minimize the anxiety levels of those in Kentucky, Polk was already plotting its invasion to serve the crucial campaign for the defense of the Mississippi River. Urged on by General Pillow, Polk claimed to have no instructions from Richmond at all with regard to a policy in Kentucky.[151] Polk took it upon himself to write to Magoffin on September 1, 1861: "I think it of the greatest consequence to the southern cause in Kentucky or elsewhere that I should be ahead of the enemy in occupying Columbus and Paducah."[152]

Therefore, while President Lincoln seemed to be attempting to rein in General Fremont in the Department of the West for his actions in Missouri, Polk was speaking with presidential policy authority by directly addressing the governor of the state of Kentucky. Jefferson Davis later agreed with the suggestions of Pillow and Polk, saying that the Confederacy had acted rightly in self-defense for the Union was certainly ready to invade. For his part, Davis's own correspondence with Magoffin had not been untrue or misleading because Davis insisted that the only thing that would preclude a Confederate military occupation was the existence of a true state of neutrality. In retrospect, this had always been impossibility, given Kentucky's significant and strategic geography.

Polk interpreted the lack of specific instruction from Richmond as authorizing him to exercise discretion. Troops under General Pillow advanced on Hickman, Kentucky, on September 3. The initial response of the Confederate government came quickly, with an order of immediate troop

Kentucky governor Beriah Magoffin, who requested that Jefferson Davis and the Confederate army recognize the neutrality of that state. Polk's detractors have argued that his hasty actions in Kentucky forced the state into the Union camp. Even President Lincoln recognized the untenable arguments about state neutrality, and Kentucky could not have hoped to maintain this posture for the duration of the war. *Courtesy of Library of Congress, Civil War Prints and Photographs Division, Washington, D.C.*

withdrawal coming from Secretary LeRoy Pope Walker. Interestingly, Polk did not respond to Walker, saying he would act only on the orders of Jefferson Davis. Davis later affirmed and wrote, "The necessity justifies the action."[153]

September 8 found Polk again penning a letter to the governor of Kentucky, this time explaining the Confederate position and justifying their presence: "The federal forces intended and were preparing to seize Columbus. I need not describe to you the danger resulting to West Tennessee from such occupation…as the Confederate troops approached this place, the Federal troops were found in formidable numbers in position upon the opposite bank, with their cannon turned on Columbus."[154]

John Johnson, chairman of a special committee of the Kentucky state legislature, responded to the Confederate invasion with a letter addressed to General Polk: "In obedience to the thrice-repeated will of the people, as expressed at the polls, and in their name, I ask you to withdraw your forces from the soil of Kentucky."[155] Polk responded to Johnson the same day, focusing not on the plaintive plea of the legislative committee but on justifying the action. Polk also used his response as an opportunity to suggest that Johnson had little authority to have written such a request in the first place: "It appears your office as committeemen was restricted merely to collecting the facts in reference to the recent occupation of Kentucky soil by the Confederate and Federal forces, and to report thereon in writing at as early a date as possible."[156]

In later correspondence with Jefferson Davis, Polk suggested that the people of Kentucky overreacted to the Confederate presence.[157]

On September 13, Governor Magoffin issued a proclamation that ordered the Confederate troops out of the state,[158] to which Jefferson Davis reacted by consulting Albert Sidney Johnston, who had recently arrived from his journey from California. Davis wrote to Polk on September 15, "Your wish for General A.S. Johnston to command the operations in the west have been fulfilled. He is now, I suppose, at Nashville, and you will soon have the aid of his presence with the army."[159] Johnston himself seems to have enjoyed the final word on the matter by writing simply to Jefferson Davis the following day: "The troops will not be withdrawn…so far from yielding to the demand for the withdrawal of our troops, I have determined to occupy Bowling Green at once."[160]

By late September, Johnston had assigned Polk to the defense of the Mississippi River, a task that originally also included the Tennessee and Cumberland Rivers. Polk seemed aware that the duty called for significantly more support and boldly wrote to Johnston insisting that other provisions be made: "I beg leave to call the attention of the commanding officer to the importance of having some commander of large experience and military efficiency put in charge of the defenses of the Tennessee and Cumberland rivers."[161] The months that followed witnessed the inconclusive Battle of Belmont on November 7, between General Pillow and General Ulysses Grant, following which Polk received minor concussion and ear injuries from standing near cannon fire. However, the same event that brought a minor injury to Polk claimed the life of one of his closest aides, Lieutenant Snowden, who had become a trusted assistant. The death of Snowden impacted Polk profoundly, as it did the rest of the troops. During this time, Polk was also arguing with Johnston and seemed determined again to leave the Confederate service. Meanwhile, the Confederate Congress in Richmond passed resolutions of commendation for Polk for his actions at Belmont. It was a challenging and conflicting time for Polk, both personally and militarily.

Before the arrival of Johnston in the western theater, Polk made executive policy with regard to Kentucky. This is something that Jefferson Davis allowed but was not traditionally within the purview of a military commander. As a result of this, Kentucky declared itself Unionist, an outcome that may have meant the loss of the war for the Confederacy. In early November, Polk offered his resignation to Jefferson Davis; some historians note that Davis should have accepted it and released him from service.[162] It is true that both Paducah and Columbus would have strengthened the Confederate line of defense in the West, but the extent to which Polk bears full responsibility is debatable. Albert Sidney Johnston arrived at a crucial time in the Kentucky campaign, and his decisions must also be factored into any complete assessment of the outcomes.

The end of 1861 found Polk in frequent correspondence with his wife, the first of which, dated November 12, focused chiefly on reporting his account of his injury at Belmont. This letter captures the event that injured Polk but also hints at his attempts to process the trauma of what must have been a frightening battle experience:

> *I write you a letter with my own hand that you may see I am safe notwithstanding the battle through which we passed on the 7th, and the terrible explosion yesterday of the Dahlgren gun carrying a 128 pound shot. I was standing within ten feet of the gun at the moment of the explosion. The captain of the company to which the squad of men serving the gun belonged was killed on the spot; so were the captain of the gun squad and*

five others, one of those being one of my aides, Lieutenant Snowden. Two of the men were blown into the river, a hundred feet below. Their bodies have not been recovered. My clothes were torn to pieces and I was literally covered with dust and fragments of the wreck. I was only injured by the stunning effect of the concussion.[163]

His Christmas letter to his wife assumed a more pastoral and reflective tone as Polk's recovery from his ruptured eardrum injury was complete:

It's Christmas Day! A day on which angels sang "Glory to God in the highest, peace on earth and good will towards men." How my heart yearns to join you in the same song, if our enemies would let us. Indeed, I may say with truth, I can and do feel the full force of the sentiment of the song towards them. Notwithstanding the warlike purposes in their hearts, I feel no unkindness toward them or toward any living being, and would bless and pray for them if they would let me. But we trust now as ever that the Lord will deliver us out of their hands, and that with a great deliverance, and give them a better mind.

In his Christmas missive at the end of the first year of the war, Polk framed his reflection scripturally and theologically but in a way that indicates he was convinced of the absolute moral correctness of the cause and the necessity for military actions until such time as the Union had "a better mind." It was a synthesis of his contrasting natures that was to be seen again and again throughout his service in the war.

The early months of 1862 were characterized by watching and waiting, with everyone quite correctly expecting that the major Union initiatives would be directed at gaining control of the Mississippi River. It was a time when Polk made yet another attempt to resign, and he seemed hopeful for a return to his previous life. Confederate volunteers were now especially difficult to come by, and morale was already suffering under the weight of a harsh winter. General Halleck became the commander of the Union forces in the West, initiating action to be led by General Curtis into Arkansas and a separate action under Generals Grant and Pope to head down the Mississippi River. For the Confederacy, General Beauregard arrived in Columbus, and Polk once again saw an opportunity to return to his previous life.

Writing his wife again, Polk said, "Beauregard has been ordered here; that suits me very well, as it will furnish the grounds of my insisting on Davis' allowing me to retire, which I have done by letter and sent to Richmond.

But this is a secret. I presume he cannot now decline."[164] However, Jefferson Davis did, in fact, decline Polk's resignation a second time. The Confederate situation was critical in early 1862, and every man's service was needed. Fort Henry had fallen, Fort Donelson was under imminent Union threat and Polk could not summon the means to abandon the cause to which he still believed he had been called as his "duty next." The year 1862 witnessed a bloody battle at a place called Shiloh and the death of Polk's friend and West Point roommate, Albert Sidney Johnston, prompting yet another turning point in plans for the Confederacy and in the personal life of Bishop-General Polk.

Chapter 7

IN THE ARMY OF TENNESSEE AND CONFLICT WITH BRAXTON BRAGG: 1862-63

"How Can One Subdue a Nation Such as This?

Throughout the action in the western theater during 1862, relations were strained between Polk and another Confederate commander, Major General Braxton Bragg. It was the year that witnessed horrific casualties for both sides at a battle that took place at Pittsburg Landing on the Tennessee River but became forever known as the Battle of Shiloh. In the aftermath of that battle, the lack of a unified and cohesive Confederate command structure in the West became obvious. At the center of the controversy was Leonidas Polk, whose actions at Shiloh and the following year at Chickamauga continue to be the subject of disagreement among military historians. Polk's own correspondence from the period serves as a framework from which to explore his ongoing difficulty with personal criticism and an underlying arrogance first seen in his West Point days as a young cadet.

On March 6, 1862, came General Orders No. 1 from the headquarters of the Army of Mississippi, which clearly stated:

> *I. Major General L. Polk will assume command of all the troops of this army north of Jackson, Tennessee, and along the Mississippi River north of Memphis. Commanders of posts, regiments, detached companies and battalions, and of brigades will report to him accordingly.*

General Braxton Bragg, commander of the Army of Tennessee. He and Polk frequently quarreled. Bragg wanted Polk court-martialed for insubordination but eventually was himself forced to resign by the end of 1863 following the loss of Chattanooga to Union forces. *Courtesy of Library of Congress, Civil War Prints and Photographs Division, Washington, D.C.*

II. Major General Braxton Bragg will assume command of all the troops of this army south of Major General Polk's command. He will at the same time retain command of his department.

III. Until further orders, Major General Bragg will issue all orders from these headquarters for the movement of troops in Western Tennessee.[165]

A Union army under General Ulysses Grant had taken up a position near Pittsburg Landing on the Tennessee River, and by the last week of March 1862, all of the Western Department was concentrated in or around the chief Union objective of Corinth, Mississippi. Corinth was a major railway hub. If Corinth fell to the Union forces, it would divide the Confederacy and cut off vital supply lines and communications links. Still known as the Army of Mississippi at this point in time, the command structure included Albert Sidney Johnston as commander in chief, P.G.T. Beauregard as second in command and Braxton Bragg as chief of staff. The army was divided into four corps in March 1862, with commands given to Polk, Bragg, William Hardee and John Breckinridge.

Right: Union general Ulysses S. Grant determined to break the Confederacy by control of the major rivers and disruption of Confederate rail service and supply lines. Following his victories in Tennessee, Grant became commander of all Union armies in March 1864. *Courtesy of Library of Congress, Civil War Prints and Photographs Division, Washington, D.C.*

Below: Shiloh Church, for which the battle was named that took place near Pittsburg Landing on the Tennessee River in March 1862. Ironically, the word *shiloh* in Hebrew means "a place of peace," but it became the site of the bloodiest battle to date in the war. It was a battle that witnessed the loss of Polk's friend General Albert Sidney Johnston. *Courtesy of Library of Congress, Civil War Prints and Photographs Division, Washington, D.C.*

With the forces of Ulysses Grant camped on the west bank of the Tennessee River, a second Federal army under General Buell was moving through Tennessee to join Grant's forces. Just two miles west of Pittsburg Landing was the tiny Shiloh Church, for which the looming battle would be named. Ironically, the word *shiloh* in Hebrew means "a place of peace," deriving from a biblical reference in Samuel 1 as a gathering point for the people of Israel. It was to become synonymous with the worst bloodshed of the Civil War to date.

These reorganized Confederate troops advanced on the Union position at Pittsburg Landing, but there appears to have been no unified coordination of the troop divisions. Johnston intended for the surprise attack to be ordered thus: Polk's division to the left, Bragg's to the center and Hardee's to the right (the corps of Breckinridge was to function as a reserve).[166] Johnston felt confident of both the structure and his commanders.

William Preston, assistant to General A.S. Johnston, wrote of the discussions regarding the readiness of the Confederate units for attack due to delays from heavy rainfall. It was a consultation in which Polk had a significant role and indicates the esteem with which Johnston regarded him:

> *The divisions of General Polk and Breckinridge came up, and a consultation was held by General Johnston with his chief officers. He informed me that someone or more doubted the propriety of attacking General Grant's forces, on account of the delay, and considered it best to withdraw to Corinth. It was then about four o'clock and after a short while, General Johnston came near and directed Colonel Jordan, serving as chief of staff, to prepare to write orders...in the course of our short conversation, he spoke in very complimentary terms of General Polk and said, "Polk is a true soldier and friend."*[167]

Johnston and Beauregard had differing plans for the same effort, but the initial assault on the Union position on April 6 was nevertheless fierce, in spite of an apparent lack of coordination. The organization and subdivision of the Confederate troops meant that Bragg had larger numbers than either Polk or Hardee; his division also had very few veterans. The resulting assault on the Union position was not sustainable beyond the first day of the battle. By the second day, the Union army had fresh reinforcements. General Beauregard also had to assume the role of commander in chief due to the death of Albert Sidney Johnston. By late afternoon on April 7, Beauregard withdrew, and Grant chose not to pursue with any significant tenacity. The

Union casualties numbered more than thirteen thousand, and Confederate losses were greater than ten thousand.

Polk's report of the battle is interesting for the light it sheds on his thoughts, ranging from the objective accounts of a general, to keen observations of humanity under pressure, to the grief of losing a friend in battle:

> *At the appointed hour of the morning of the 6ᵗʰ, my troops were moved forward and so soon as they were freed from an obstruction formed by a thicket of underbrush, they were formed in column of brigades and pressed onward to the support of the second line. General Clark's division was in front. We had not proceeded far before the first line, under General Hardee, was under fire throughout its length, and the second, under General Bragg, was also engaged.*

Polk interestingly took notice of the courage of the enemy in his report: "The resistance at this point was as stubborn as at any other on the field. The forces of the enemy to which we were opposed were understood to be those of General Sherman, supported by the command of General McClernand. They fought with determined courage, and contested every inch of ground."

The same report also included a poignant account of the fall of his friend Albert Sidney Johnston:

> *About three o'clock intelligence reached me that the commander in chief, General Johnston, had fallen. He fell in discharge of his duty, leading and directing his troops. His loss was deeply felt. It was an event which deprived the army of his clear, practical judgment and determined character, and himself of an opportunity he had courted for vindicating his claims to the confidence of his countrymen against the inconsiderate and unjust reproaches which had been heaped upon him…he was a true soldier, high-toned, eminently honorable and just, considerate of the rights and feelings of others, magnanimous and brave. His military capacity was also of a high order, and his devotion to the cause of the South unsurpassed by that of any of her noble sons who had offered up their lives on her altar. I knew him well from childhood—none knew him better—and I take pleasure in laying on his tomb as a parting offering this testimonial of my appreciation of his character as a soldier, a patriot and a man.*[168]

Polk's strong written defense of Albert Sidney Johnston derived, at least in part, from the recent very public efforts to remove Johnston from

Union general John McClernand, who commanded a corps at the Battle of Shiloh in action against Polk's troops. Like Polk, McClernand had led a very different life before the war; he served as both a journalist and a United States representative from Illinois before the war broke out. *Courtesy of Library of Congress, Civil War Prints and Photographs Division, Washington, D.C.*

The tree at Shiloh where Albert Sidney Johnston is said to have fallen when mortally wounded. The tree trunk was preserved for its symbolic association. This photograph was taken in 1999. *Courtesy of Library of Congress, Civil War Prints and Photographs Division, Washington, D.C.*

command in the West. In early March, Representative E.M. Bruce from Kentucky wrote to Jefferson Davis and implored him to remove Johnston from command and replace him with Bragg, Beauregard or Breckinridge. Bruce reported to Davis that his negative opinion of Johnston was "almost unanimous" among "officers, soldiers, and citizens." The congressman ended his letter to Davis with the dramatic appeal of "Save us while it is yet time."[169]

Polk also wrote to his wife a few days after the battle, expressing his gratitude for surviving the battle but also clearly impressed with the excitement of the day:

> *I am thankful to say that the protecting hand of God was over me and around me, and I experienced no harm during either of the two days of the battle, although I was in the thickest of the storm during both days. All glory and honor be unto His holy name for my protection and defense, for it was He who did it. It was He who "covered my head in the day of battle." I cannot describe the field. It was one of great carnage, and as it was the second battle I had been in—the other being a bloody one also—I*

felt somewhat more accustomed to it. This one was on a larger scale, and a magnificent affair.[170]

This correspondence underscores the contradictions of Polk as a historical figure. He was known by officers and enlisted men alike as a bishop, and much can be said for his presence on the battlefield as a calming influence. There can be no question that his presence inspired a general feeling of well-being for the troops with him or near him. However, the nature of the roles often made it difficult to function simultaneously as both bishop and general, as demonstrated in several incidents throughout the war. Although he seems to have struggled throughout the time of his military service with outward expressions of his Episcopal office, all of his personal correspondence continued to reflect a deep and profound personal faith, as seen in the correspondence with Frances. Polk believed in the omnipresence of God and in the military duty to which he was called. He also remained convinced of the righteousness of the Southern cause and linked it to his personal faith in a remarkable blend of patriotic religious zeal.

After the Battle of Shiloh, the Confederate military focus shifted to stopping Union progress in the Mississippi River Valley and especially on the immediate priority of losing no further ground in Tennessee. It was at this point that Braxton Bragg replaced Beauregard in what became the Army of Tennessee. Polk did not like Bragg and, in fact, saw him as an incompetent commander. Throughout the next year, Polk campaigned more than once to have Bragg removed from his command. However, the feeling was mutual; Bragg shared a similar view of Polk's level of competence as a field commander. It was a mutual enmity that would have divisive consequences for the Confederate war effort over the coming months.

Bragg believed that an offensive against Union troops in Tennessee was necessary, and to aid in this endeavor was Edmund Kirby Smith, who was to work on dislodging the Union presence from the Cumberland Gap. Because Smith was unsuccessful, he instead turned his attention to Lexington, Kentucky, and Bragg made the decision to follow him. The two men abandoned what had already been agreed upon to be the wisest course of immediate action—to rid the Mississippi River Valley of Union forces.

Some historians have said that at this very critical time, Bragg and Smith both fell victim to "Kentucky Fever." The term referred to the zeal with which many Southerners seem to have believed that Kentucky could actually be won over to the Confederate cause, even after Polk's invasion turned the tide of that sympathy a year before. Bragg even boldly informed the citizens

Confederate lieutenant general Edmund Kirby Smith, who planned an invasion of Kentucky with Braxton Bragg. Historians often suggest that Smith and Bragg both suffered from what became known as "Kentucky Fever," the idea that Kentucky would be moved from its position of neutrality to support the Confederate cause.
Courtesy of Library of Congress, Civil War Prints and Photographs Division, Washington, D.C.

of Kentucky, "The Army of Tennessee offers you an opportunity to free yourselves from the tyranny of a despotic ruler."[171]

The Kentucky Campaign was flawed, again due to a lack of coordination that now seemed endemic to the Confederate army in the west. Both Bragg and Kirby Smith operated independently. Bragg finally made the decision to withdraw from Kentucky, after which opinion of him among many in the Confederate army and command structure began to dramatically decline. This included the man who would become one of Bragg's most ardent critics—Leonidas Polk.

How much of Polk's opinion is based on honest criticism of Bragg's ability cannot be known in light of other events. Bragg accused Polk of disobedience on multiple occasions leading up to their final showdown after the Battle of Chickamauga in September 1863. At Bardstown in October 1862, Polk disobeyed an order of Bragg's when he realized that his corps would be surrounded. Polk had done something similar at Perryville, again earning Bragg's sharp rebuke. In fact, Bragg laid the blame on Polk for the entire failure of the Army of Tennessee and, by the following year, was hopeful that Davis would not only relieve Polk of duty but would also court-martial him.[172] It is interesting to note that Polk's promotion to lieutenant general became effective on October 10, 1862.

Polk's posture in response to Bragg was one of confidence bordering on arrogance. He was always careful to avoid the use of the term "disobedience" in his responses to Bragg's accusations. His justifications for his insubordination are not unlike those that were seen as a cadet at West Point. Polk was a man who had difficulty processing any degree of criticism, and a self-righteous indignation generally resulted from any perceived impingement on his personal honor or integrity. Polk tried on a few occasions to dislodge Bragg from his command post, calling on his friend Jefferson Davis.[173]

From this period emerges an amusing anecdote. At the Battle of Perryville, the fading light of day made it difficult to distinguish the color of Federal and Confederate uniforms. Polk observed a unit he believed to be wearing gray firing on a Confederate position. Polk approached the unit commander and demanded that the incident of "friendly fire" cease immediately. He even asked of the commander, "What is your name, sir?" To this, the officer respectfully responded, "Colonel Shyrock, of the Eighty-seventh Indiana." Polk realized he was among the enemy but bluffed his position well. Shaking his fist at the colonel, Polk shouted, "Cease firing at once!" Polk then mustered the authority to sit tall in his saddle and ride away. He later recalled the great anxiety he felt in those few moments, certain he might be identified as a Confederate general before he made it safely away.[174] This incident may have been the inspiration for Polk riding with Confederate chaplain C.T. Quintard (who later also became a bishop) to a nearby Episcopal church in Harrodsburg, where Polk knelt at the altar and wept.[175]

Morale was low for the Confederate army; it was an issue of which Bragg was well aware, even early in 1863 when he issued a circular letter to his commanders directly addressing the negative talk about him in a thinly veiled accusation that surely included Polk:

> It has come to my knowledge that many of these accusations and insinuations are from staff officers of my generals, who persistently assert that the movement was made against the opinion and advice of their chiefs, and while the enemy was in full retreat. False or true, the soldiers have no means of judging me rightly, or getting the facts, and the effect on them will be the same—a loss of confidence, and a consequent demoralization of the whole army.[176]

Correspondence throughout the period in question reveals the tension that existed within Bragg's command structure in the Army of Tennessee. Nevertheless, in a letter to his wife dated March 30, 1863, Polk was full of pride for his men upon a visit by Jefferson Davis's aide-de-camp and again reflects the moral correctness with which he viewed the concept of rebellion:

> It was a fine affair, and all things went off satisfactorily. The troops looked very well, and I never saw them march so well. My corps was never in better condition, and is now about 20,000 strong. I confess I felt proud of the fellows as they marched by me today. In their hearts is embodied as large and as intense an amount of rebellion as ever was concentrated in the same number of men.[177]

By this time, Polk's Southern nationalism had found full expression within his theological worldview. The transformation from bishop to general, never easy and occasionally wrought with logistical difficulties, was complete through a process of fusion. It may be an important factor in understanding the depth and extent of Polk's convictions, even as they touched on the military actions of the Confederate army.

On the occasion of his fifty-seventh birthday, Polk again wrote to Frances of an impending visit from Bragg to inspect his troops at Shelbyville. The letter finds Polk reflective of his military service and hinting at the conflict with Bragg. Yet again, it is all framed within the terms of Polk's personal faith: "Just to think, I am fifty-seven! I have spent many of these years as I would not again. But in many of them I have tried to do my duty. The Lord pardon the omissions of the past and give me the grace to redeem the time in the future."[178]

The dual roles of Polk inspired curiosity and fascination in others who met him during this time. In the summer of 1863, Polk met English lieutenant colonel Arthur L. Fremantle, who recorded his meeting with Polk by noting:

> *Lieutenant-General Leonidas Polk, Bishop of Louisiana, who commands the other corps d'armee, is a good looking, gentleman-like man, with all the manners and affability of a "grand seigneur." He is fifty-seven years of age, tall, upright, and looks much more the soldier than the clergyman. He is much beloved by the soldiers on account of his great personal courage and agreeable manners. I had already heard no end of anecdotes about him, told me by my travelling companions, who always alluded to him with affection and admiration. In his clerical capacity, I had always heard him spoken of with the greatest respect.*[179]

During his visit to the Confederacy in 1863, Fremantle also revealed further insights regarding the depth of Polk's personal faith and his dedication to the Southern cause. Upon hearing of a widow who had lost three sons in the Confederate army and had only one son of sixteen years of age remaining, Polk went to see her to offer spiritual comfort. The grieving mother looked at Polk and promised that her remaining son would serve too. Fremantle recalled Polk's eyes watering with tears as he said, "How can one subdue a nation such as this?"[180]

There are other records of Polk functioning as a bishop in the sphere of military action. Before the Atlanta Campaign (which would claim his own life), Polk baptized John Q. Hood, Joseph Johnston and William Hardee. Also, Polk was present as pastor at the bedside of Major Edward Butler, who was mortally wounded at the Battle of Belmont in November 1861. In December 1862, Polk presided at the wedding of Colonel John Morgan a few days before the Battle of Stone's River.[181] There are doubtlessly other such events that are not documented.

It is an especially interesting intersection of history that during the early summer of 1863, a time of enmity between Polk and Bragg, Bragg received the Christian rites of baptism and confirmation from Polk's visiting friend Stephen Elliott, the bishop of Georgia. Bragg and Polk shook hands following the ceremony[182] and unquestionably were able to see the higher calling of the occasion. Having a religious presence in the army did sometimes inspire men to rise above the events about them. Shortly after this event, Polk wrote to Frances, observing the necessity of meeting these religious needs of the army. Once again, Polk assumed the role of a bishop of the church yet couched his observations equally within his Southern patriotism:

> *A great and highly commendable effort is now being made by the religious bodies of the country to supply the spiritual wants of the army, and I hope the best results will follow from their effort. It is one in which I take great interest, and which I foster in every way in my power. Indeed, I think on the judicious application of the means of imparting religious instruction to the army very much depends the future condition of our people when it shall please God to relieve us from the pressure of this scourging war and restore us to peace.* [183]

During that summer of 1863, the religious attention given to the troops could only help the anxiety levels, for the early July losses at Vicksburg and Gettysburg proved to be great blows to Confederate morale. Efforts in Tennessee only deteriorated with personal consequences for General Polk. At the Battle of Chickamauga near Chattanooga on September 19, Bragg's strategy involved giving command of a critical aspect to Polk. Although the battle might have been a tactical victory for the Confederacy, it was a failure for Bragg because Union commander William Rosecrans managed to escape with a large portion of his army.[184] Interestingly, the battle also marked the end of Rosecrans's military career under the pall of harsh scrutiny.

The Battle of Chickamauga became another opportunity for Bragg to blame Polk. Because of Polk's failure to follow orders and attack at sunrise, Bragg suspended him from duty and ordered him to Atlanta, and it appeared for a while that Polk was to be court-martialed. Polk immediately appealed to his friend Jefferson Davis with a version of events that not only overtly disputes Bragg but also defends Polk's decision to go against the orders of a superior officer:

> *Two days subsequent to my writing this letter to you, I received an order from General Bragg suspending me from my command and ordering me to this place. This order was based on alleged disobedience in not attacking the enemy at daylight on Sunday the 20th. My explanation of that failure was furnished in a note, of which the accompanying is a copy...for the*

Above: *The Battle of Chickamauga.* This drawing by Alfred Waud shows the Confederate line advancing. The battle might have been a tactical victory for the Confederacy and temporarily boosted morale, but it was short-lived. Bragg cited Polk for insubordination following this battle and urged his court-martial, but Jefferson Davis declined. *Courtesy of Library of Congress, Civil War Prints and Photographs Division, Washington, D.C.*

Left: Union general William Rosecrans, whose military career also ended after the Battle of Chickamauga. *Courtesy of Library of Congress, Civil War Prints and Photographs Division, Washington, D.C.*

Photograph of Chickamauga Creek, circa 1860–65. *Courtesy of Library of Congress, Civil War Prints and Photographs Division, Washington, D.C.*

delay charged I cannot feel myself responsible, and it should be observed, by whomsoever caused, it did not occasion any failure in our success in the battle, for the enemy was clearly beaten at all points along my line and fairly driven from the field. It will no doubt be affirmed that had the attack been made at daylight the enemy would have been overwhelmed, Chattanooga taken, etc., etc…and that all subsequent delays and miscarriages are to be set down to that account. To make this affirmation good it must be shown that at the close of the battle that night such a condition of things was developed as to make pursuit impossible, and that it was equally hopeless next morning.[185]

At the end of the letter, Polk summed up his weariness with dealing with Braxton Bragg by concluding with a note of resignation, "My experience in this army has taught me to expect such a movement at any time for the last two years. I am not, therefore, taken by surprise. I have respectfully asked of the Secretary of War a court of inquiry at the earliest moment."[186]

Chattanooga at the Tennessee River, circa 1863. This was a strategically crucial position for the Union forces from which to begin the Atlanta Campaign. *Courtesy of Library of Congress, Civil War Prints and Photographs Division, Washington, D.C.*

Jefferson Davis realized that to court-martial Polk would be to invite unnecessary controversy and division at a time when Confederate morale was at its lowest. Instead, Davis transferred Polk to Mississippi, and Bragg did eventually resign his command, in disgrace, in November 1863 following a rout of the Army of Tennessee at Chattanooga. Following this series of battles that were quite costly for the Confederate armies, Bragg attempted to lay the blame on Breckinridge. When Bragg tendered his resignation to Jefferson Davis, he was likely both surprised and disappointed that Davis accepted it immediately. The Union now controlled Tennessee, and the city of Chattanooga became a base of operations for the Union's forthcoming Atlanta Campaign.

Confederate prisoners at the depot in Chattanooga, 1863. Following the final battles of Chattanooga (the Chattanooga Campaign of November 1863), Jefferson Davis removed Braxton Bragg from command of the Army of Tennessee, replacing him with Joseph Johnston. This transfer meant General Polk's return, briefly, to the Army of Tennessee. *Courtesy of Library of Congress, Civil War Prints and Photographs Division, Washington, D.C.*

Polk assumed a new command in December 1863, responsible for the Department of Mississippi and East Louisiana, at the beginning of what would prove to be the last chapter of his life. Yet he began the new and final command with an even more pronounced sense of what was best for the Confederacy. Upon hearing the news of Bragg's resignation, his correspondence with Jefferson Davis made ever-bolder suggestions about the command of the Army of Tennessee. Calling on "the frankness of the intercourse which has characterized our long acquaintance," Polk pushed Davis to offer the command to General Joseph Johnston.[187] That Polk took such liberties in his correspondence with Davis is at

Left: Confederate general Joseph Johnston, to whom command of the Army of Tennessee was assigned following the removal of Braxton Bragg at the end of 1863. It was Johnston who summoned General Polk to reconnoiter Union positions near Pine Mountain on a fateful morning in June 1864 when Polk was mortally wounded. *Courtesy of Library of Congress, Civil War Prints and Photographs Division, Washington, D.C.*

Right: General Robert E. Lee, the most capable of the Confederate generals, responsible for the Army of Northern Virginia. Lee and Polk were classmates at West Point Academy. *Courtesy of Library of Congress, Civil War Prints and Photographs Division, Washington, D.C.*

once understandable yet inappropriate. The relationships between the men of the Confederacy, old acquaintances from their days at West Point, contributed to a familiarity that went beyond propriety in a centralized command structure. This resulted in repeated courses of action that may not have always best served the overall objectives.

So it was that the new year of 1864 dawned, finding Leonidas Polk in a new command, with new controversies, and ushering in the last months of his life.

Chapter 8

THE DEATH AND LEGACY OF
THE BISHOP-GENERAL

"His Example Is before You; His Mantle Rests with You"

With General Joseph Johnston as replacement for Braxton Bragg, Polk briefly rejoined the Army of Tennessee. The appointment of Johnston to Bragg's previous post had not been an easy one for Jefferson Davis to make, because the two men had quarreled frequently from the beginning of the war. There was a mutual dislike between the men; however, the fact that Johnston was an outsider to the Army of Tennessee made him an attractive choice given the state of political turmoil and division within its ranks. By this time, the Union objective was to take the city of Atlanta, and the best possible commander was needed to respond.

The Atlanta Campaign was the most important of the actions to date in the western theater of the war. Ulysses Grant, recently promoted to general in chief, planned to cut off the Confederacy by disabling army and supply movements between east and west.[188] This led to a campaign throughout 1864 that raged through the hills and mountains of Georgia, one that frustrated the Confederate army, exposed grave deficiencies in the response of the Confederate president and command structure and brought general despair to the people of Georgia. It would also take the life of Leonidas Polk.

By this time, the war had raged for three years, far beyond what anyone might have imagined at its outset in 1861. Many throughout the Deep South were despondent and weary of war, almost in a state of accepting defeat as the ideal of the "lost cause" began to take shape. Many in the North had not been in favor of using force to keep the seceded states in the Union in the first place, and these voices grew only louder with the passage of time and the climbing death toll. The cost in human lives had been more than many could stomach, to say nothing of the mounting financial costs of the war. Observers and reporters were already hailing the crushing Confederate defeats of 1863 as having effectively turned the tide of the war in favor of the Union. Therefore, the Union planned the campaign of 1864 to serve as the death knell for the Confederacy, to break its will and resistance and to divide the Confederacy yet again.

Because the Confederacy had always been inferior in numbers, ease of supply and maintaining a state of ready mobility throughout the Mississippi River Valley had always been a key part of the overall military strategy. Confederate troops could respond where they were needed, so keeping soldiers mobile was a means of attempting to compensate for the numerical advantage of the Union armies.[189] General Grant knew this, of course, and understood that a strategy of assaulting the Confederacy at multiple points simultaneously could bring a speedy conclusion to the conflict. One of the points of attack was from Chattanooga to Atlanta and, ultimately, the Gulf of Mexico. To this task was charged General William Tecumseh Sherman.

General Sherman knew that a key question of the planned Atlanta Campaign was the availability of supplies. He knew his supply lines were long and vulnerable, and this led him to order that each man had to carry on his person enough food for five days but relieved them of the obligation of carrying what he believed to be unnecessary equipment such as tents and wagons. This created maximum maneuverability for the Union army marching into Georgia. It also meant, of course, that Sherman's troops would depend on the goods, products and resources of the local population—a tactic that reinforced the overall goal of breaking whatever vestiges of resistance remained in the Deep South.

From May to September 1864, the two sides were engaged in almost constant combat. General Sherman took nearly 100,000 Union troops heading into Georgia, and Johnston could manage only about 70,000. This meant Johnston would have to rely on a strategy of avoiding direct battle whenever possible, instead opting for limited engagements that would maximize troop survival and available resources. Such a strategy demanded intricate knowledge of the enemy, yet one of the greatest weaknesses of the Confederate military at this point in time was the lack of reliable intelligence about Union activity and numbers in Georgia. This lack of information may

Union general William Tecumseh Sherman, who carried out the significant Atlanta Campaign in 1864, during which Polk was killed by Union artillery fire. *Courtesy of Library of Congress, Civil War Prints and Photographs Division, Washington, D.C.*

have been due to ineffective use of available cavalry for scouting purposes,[190] a matter that proved to have costly consequences. These details provide important background for the circumstances leading to Polk's death, as he responded to a final request from his commanding officer, Joseph Johnston. It was a request that may have never been if Johnston had been in possession of adequate intelligence.

The situation in Georgia was worsened by the almost complete deterioration in communications at the highest levels of the Confederate government and command structure by early 1864. When Sherman's advance became known in Richmond, Bragg ordered Polk to send an entire infantry division to Johnston as support in Alabama, while Jefferson Davis ordered Polk to move all troops to Johnston's defense in Alabama.[191] Davis allowed Bragg to save face after his resignation from the Army of Tennessee by giving him a staff position in Richmond and then seemed to not communicate with Bragg at all.

Johnston's necessary strategy of maintaining troop mobility is what dominated the Confederate response to the Atlanta Campaign. Johnston chose to consistently concentrate his forces on the best available terrain and limit actual engagement with Sherman's forces, thereby preserving an outward posture of readiness. Sherman used this to his advantage by forcing Johnston to repeatedly move and construct or find new defenses. For over a month, the armies gradually moved deeper into Georgia, and the campaign became one of maneuver for both sides.

It was the need to sustain this strategy that prompted Johnston's consultation with Polk atop Pine Mountain. On the morning of June 13, Johnston sent a message to Polk requesting his presence and opinion regarding "the mode of occupying our entrenchments to the best advantage."[192] Johnston made clear in his message that it was crucial to maintain the mobility of their limited forces, asking that Polk render an opinion regarding the minimum number of men and guns necessary. The two men exchanged further correspondence that day, and Polk met with Johnston that evening, when the men agreed to meet the next day to examine the position of Union forces under Major General Bate near Pine Mountain.

On that fateful morning of June 14, Johnston, Hardee and Polk joined together for the reconnaissance, and the surrounding topography provided opportunity for observing the Union positions. The men rode to the summit of nearby Pine Mountain to further develop a plan predicated on Johnston's need to conserve troop mobility. Suddenly, Union artillery fire began, and Polk was struck in the chest by a three-inch ball that ripped directly through

Death of General Polk on Pine Mountain, drawing created by Alfred Waud, 1864. Polk was struck directly in the chest by Union artillery fire on June 14, 1864, killing him instantly. *Courtesy of Library of Congress, Civil War Prints and Photographs Division, Washington, D.C.*

him before striking a nearby tree and exploding. Polk was killed instantly. The first men to reach Polk's side were staff members Lieutenant Aristide Hopkins and Colonel W.D. Gale, both of whom gave accounts of what they witnessed, and both of whom had attempted to warn him of the imminent danger of his bold stance in open view. General Johnston knelt by his fallen friend and wept, saying, "I would rather anything but this."[193]

His son William Mecklenburg Polk eloquently described the death scene in his father's biography: "Folding his arm across his breast, he stood intently gazing upon the scene below. While he thus stood, a cannon-shot crashed through his breast, and opening a wide door, let free that indomitable spirit."[194]

Private Sam Rush Watkins of the First Tennessee Regiment gave an eyewitness account of Polk's death:

> *A solid shot from the Federal guns struck him on his left breast, passing through his body and through his heart. I saw him while the infirmary corps were bringing him off the field. He was as white as a piece of marble, and a most remarkable thing about him was that not a drop of blood was ever seen to come out of the place through which the cannon ball had passed. My pen and ability is inadequate to the task of doing his memory justice. Every private soldier loved him. Second to Stonewall Jackson, his loss was the greatest the South ever sustained.[195]*

Word spread quickly throughout the camp of the death of the bishop-general. That afternoon came General Field Order No. 2 from the commanding general of the Army of Tennessee, which assumed the form of a fitting elegy—a tribute that helped to quickly anchor in history the image of Leonidas Polk as a patriot-martyr and made complete Polk's fusion as a soldier-saint:

> *Comrades, you are called to mourn your first captain, your oldest companion in arms, Lieutenant-General Polk fell today at the outpost of this army— the army he raised and commanded, in all of whose trials he shared, to all of whose victories he contributed, in this distinquished leader we have lost the most courteous of gentlemen, the most gallant of soldiers. The Christian, patriot, soldier, has neither lived or died in vain. His example is before you; his mantle rests with you.[196]*

The end of Polk's story remains untold without the accounting of the rest of the Army of Tennessee, for which he had given his effort and his life. Unfortunately for the grieving army, the presence of Sherman's forces meant that the Confederates had very little time to mourn their fallen general and chief pastor. On June 18, Johnston withdrew from the position at Pine

Kennesaw Mountain, Georgia, the site of a major battle following Polk's death in June 1864, part of General Sherman's Atlanta Campaign. Photograph circa 1861–65. *Courtesy of Library of Congress, Civil War Prints and Photographs Division, Washington, D.C.*

Mountain into newly constructed defenses along the ridge of Kennesaw Mountain near Marietta. Sherman continued his strategy here of avoiding a full frontal assault on the Confederate position, choosing instead to continue the flanking maneuvers that had always successfully forced Johnston into moving and building new defenses. The Confederate intelligence again was faulty, and Sherman managed to cut off Johnston's ability to retreat, resulting in a skirmish at Kolb's Farm that cost Johnston much-needed men. Confederate forces available to thwart Sherman's advance now numbered only approximately forty-three thousand.[197]

The Battle of Kennesaw Mountain, which took place on June 27, was a tactical success for the Confederacy, but Johnston's success did not last long. Sherman temporarily abandoned the use of flanking maneuvers at Kennesaw, perhaps to keep Johnston guessing as to which tactic he might use. At the end of the battle, Sherman was still able to move past the Confederate entrenchments and continue his march to Atlanta in spite

Christ Church Episcopal Cathedral in New Orleans, Louisiana, Bishop General Polk's final resting place. His body was moved here after the war was over. *Courtesy of Christ Church Cathedral, Episcopal Diocese of Louisiana.*

of his initial battle plan going awry and losing nearly three thousand men. By July 2, Johnston had no choice but to withdraw from Kennesaw and return to a strategy of maneuver. As for Sherman, he was able to gift President Lincoln with the capture of Atlanta in time for the November 1864 election.

The ferocity of the Atlanta Campaign meant that Leonidas Polk was quickly mourned but also that his final rest would be delayed. After a military honor guard escort to St. Luke's Church in Atlanta, his funeral took place at St. Paul's in Augusta. This was also to be Polk's first burial; his body stayed there until the war ended and his remains could be returned to Christ Church Cathedral in New Orleans.

The Death and Legacy of the Bishop-General

Bishop Stephen Elliott of Georgia, Polk's good friend, delivered the elegy, which was not only an opportunity to memorialize his friend but also presented a political opportunity of sorts from which Elliott could expound about the Confederate cause. Elliott again linked the concepts of patriotic zeal to battlefield martyrdom. The bishop of Georgia framed his remarks with several references to Polk's sacrifice—with all the rhetoric befitting the martyrdom of the early Christian saints. Elliott characterized the war that yet raged between North and South as a fight between the forces of good and evil, between the righteous and the damned. Blaming the Union for the "murder" of Polk, Elliott further set in motion a reaction throughout the South that would perpetuate the memory of Leonidas Polk as the proto-martyr of the Confederacy.

Soon after Polk's death, the Diocesan Council of the Episcopal Diocese of Mississippi passed a resolution to pay honor and tribute to both Bishop Polk and Bishop Otey of Tennessee, who had died in April 1863. Within the resolution, the council referred to Polk as "the Senior Bishop of the Church in the Confederate States and the first Chancellor of the University of the South" and also as "a self-denying and laborious Apostle of Christ."[198] The language of the resolution links the Confederate cause and patriotism to Christian obedience by implying that Polk denied himself to serve his country and his Lord.

Any attempts to evaluate Polk or examine his legacy involve acknowledging that his life became inextricably linked to the great myth of the age that immediately followed him. The lost cause of the Confederacy became an expression of southern identity in the years after the Civil War. The South had not only been invaded and soundly defeated by Federal troops but also had its social and economic infrastructure destroyed. Historian James McPherson succinctly stated the degree of devastation by pointing out that southern wealth decreased by a staggering 60 percent.[199] Beginning at war's end in 1865, ex-Confederates needed to know that their effort had meaning and that the numbers of dead had not been in vain. The defeat had to be remembered in a way that placed it in the best light of history; hence, the lost cause quickly became a romanticized part of Civil War memory. Every cause must have its fallen heroes.

While the memory of the lost cause has faded with the passage of time, there remains the challenge of placing a figure such as Polk in a historical framework that is true to both aspects of the man—acknowledging his zeal for the political and military cause of Confederate nationalism and his love of God and the Episcopal Church. As pointed out earlier, this has proved

Confederate War Dead (1865 commemorative print) showing General Leonidas Polk. *Courtesy of Library of Congress, Civil War Prints and Photographs Division, Washington, D.C.*

to be a difficult task, as the Episcopal Church today nurses a love-hate relationship with Polk. He was a man who did more to establish a strong Episcopal presence in new areas of the United States than anyone before or since, yet he has the unfortunate taint of a secessionist cause inevitably linked to a landed slave-owning aristocracy.

There can be no question that his church-planting and commitment to evangelism represent Christian ideals to inspire any who would follow in his footsteps. His work as a bishop of the church can draw scrutiny only because of the readiness with which he left his diocese to wage war. Even then, Polk's position as general is perhaps easier to reconcile to the progressive twenty-first century than his position as slaveholder. There is the bull's-eye of historical critique—a certainty the historian must confront with a perspective framed by the norms of the age in which Polk lived. The great irony is precisely, in fact, one of perspective—for his day, Leonidas Polk was a progressive within the Episcopal Church and might have been judged liberal by his contemporaries.

Bishop-General Leonidas Polk will continue to invite examination and exploration within the contexts of military, social and religious history of the United States. Opinions of him will be as varied as the disciplines of scholars who are drawn to his story. His legacy will continue to unfold as part of the complex story of American Christianity, particularly in areas of the country where his presence represented the first non–Roman Catholic expression of the faith. There is much more to the Fighting Bishop than either his sword or his bishop's gown, as the future will most certainly reveal.

NOTES

CHAPTER 1

1. Robins, *Bishop of the Old South*, xv.
2. The idea of a moral "soldier-saint" was comprehensively explored in Southard's "Southern Soldier-Saint," 39–46.
3. *Episcopal Life Magazine*, September 2006.
4. Historical Marker Society of America: St. Philip's Episcopal Church, Harrodsburg, Kentucky.
5. Letter of Leonidas Polk, 5 June 1863, Polk papers.

CHAPTER 2

6. Robins, *Bishop of the Old South*, 1.
7. Polk, *Leonidas Polk*, vol. I, 1.
8. Writers and historians have disputed the authenticity of the Mecklenburg Declaration since the late eighteenth century, notably including a 1905 polemic work by William Henry Hoyt (*The Mecklenburg Declaration of Independence: A Study of Evidence*). The controversy over the document's authenticity did not impede the Polk family from promoting this claim.

9. Robins, *Bishop of the Old South*, 3.

10. Ibid., 4.

11. Loveland, *Emblem of Liberty*, 7.

12. Polk, *Leonidas Polk*, vol. I, 96.

13. Chorley, *Men and Movements*, 159.

14. Ibid., 146.

15. Perry, *Episcopate in America*, 75.

16. Leonidas Polk to Mary Polk, 21 June 1821, Polk papers.

17. Leonidas Polk to William Polk, 10 March 1823, Polk papers.

18. Ambrose, *Duty, Honor, Country*, 63.

19. Ibid., 71.

20. Polk, *Leonidas Polk*, vol. I, 69.

21. Leonidas Polk to William Polk, Polk papers.

22. Polk, *Leonidas Polk*, vol. I, 70.

23. Ibid., 79.

24. McIlvaine, *Memoirs*, 19.

25. Ibid., 27.

26. Polk, *Leonidas Polk*, vol. I, 90.

27. Ibid., 91.

28. McIlvaine, *Memoirs*, 210.

29. William Polk to Leonidas Polk, Polk papers.

30. Polk, *Leonidas Polk*, vol. I, 98.

31. McIlvaine, *Memoirs*, 39.

32. Leonidas Polk to William Polk, Polk papers.

33. Ibid.

34. Polk, *Leonidas Polk*, vol. I, 101.

35. Robins, *Bishop of the Old South*, 38.

36. Ibid., 39.

37. Polk, *Leonidas Polk*, vol. I, 108.

38. Ibid., 114.

39. Ibid., 121.

40. Ibid., 124.

CHAPTER 3

41. After independence from Britain, the Church of England presence in the United States adopted the name of "Episcopal" to signify governance by bishops; the word "Protestant" was a descriptor meant to distinguish it from other episcopal-

governed churches such as Roman Catholicism. The word "Protestant" has since been dropped from the formal title of the Episcopal Church.

42. Holmes, *Brief History of the Episcopal Church*, 20.

43. Posey, "Protestant Episcopal Church," 7.

44. Ibid., 7.

45. Ibid., 12.

46. Bacon, *History of American Christianity*, 210.

47. Holmes, *Brief History of the Episcopal Church*, 34.

48. Posey, "Protestant Episcopal Church," 14.

49. Polk, *Leonidas Polk*, vol. I, 145.

50. Leonidas Polk to Sarah Polk, Polk papers.

51. Ibid.

52. Armentrout, *James Hervey Otey*, 38.

53. Robins, *Bishop of the Old South*, 48.

54. Armentrout, *James Hervey Otey*, 144.

55. Otey, *Preaching the Gospel*.

56. Polk, *Leonidas Polk*, vol. I, 153.

57. Robins, *Bishop of the Old South*, 50.

58. Holmes, *Brief History of the Episcopal Church*, 65.

59. Polk, *Leonidas Polk*, vol. I, 159.

60. Robins, *Bishop of the Old South*, 87.

61. Wall, *Louisiana*, 155.

62. Follett, *Sugar Masters*, 26.

63. Wall, *Louisiana*, 155.

64. Robins, *Bishop of the Old South*, 93.

65. Ibid., 94.

66. Polk, *Leonidas Polk*, vol. I, 204.

67. Ibid., 205.

68. United States Census, 1840.

69. Polk, *Leonidas Polk*, vol. I, 183.

70. United States Census, 1850.

71. Robins, *Bishop of the Old South*, 96.

72. Polk, *Leonidas Polk*, vol. I, 184.

73. Ibid., 185.

74. Ibid., 208–9.

Chapter 4

75. Finklen and King, *History of Louisiana*, 195.
76. Ibid., 196.
77. Carrigan, "Impact of Yellow Fever," 16.
78. Duffy, *Rudolph Matas' History*, 126.
79. Ibid., 132.
80. Leonidas Polk to Stephen Elliott, 12 October 1855, Polk papers.
81. Duffy, *Rudolph Matas' History*, 21.
82. Ibid., 9.
83. Ibid., 22.
84. *Daily Picayune*, August 24, 1853.
85. Duffy, *Rudolph Matas' History*, 133.
86. Boles, *Masters and Slaves*, 25.
87. Ibid., 31.
88. Yeatman, "St. John's," 344–57.
89. Robins, *Bishop of the Old South*, 105.
90. Polk, *Leonidas Polk*, vol. I, 198.
91. Ibid., 199.
92. Butler, *Standing Against the Whirlwind*, 126.
93. Ibid., 127.
94. Polk, *Leonidas Polk*, vol. I, 209.
95. Quoted in Polk, *Leonidas Polk*, vol. I, 210.
96. Posey, "Protestant Episcopal Church," 8.
97. Green, *Memoir of Rt. Rev. James Hervey Otey*, 66.
98. Episcopal Church, *Journal of the Proceedings*, 437.
99. Ibid., 446.
100. Holmes, *Brief History of the Episcopal Church*, 117.
101. Freehling, *Road To Disunion*, 61.

Chapter 5

102. Polk, *Leonidas Polk*, vol. II, 322.
103. Robins, *Bishop of the Old South*, 142.
104. Ibid., 143.
105. Leonidas Polk to President James Buchanan, 26 December 1860, Polk papers.
106. Wall, *Louisiana*, 197.
107. Winters, *Civil War in Louisiana*, 4.
108. Ibid., 5.

109. Ibid., 7.
110. Wall, *Louisiana*, 197.
111. Polk, *Leonidas Polk*, vol. II, 302.
112. Leonidas Polk to Clergy, Episcopal Diocese of Louisiana, 30 December 1860, Polk papers.
113. Leonidas Polk to Clergy, Episcopal Diocese of Louisiana, 30 January 1861, Polk papers.
114. Ibid.
115. Polk, *Leonidas Polk*, vol. II, 317.
116. Ibid.
117. Leonidas Polk to Frances Devereux Polk, 26 April 1861, Polk papers.
118. Polk, *Leonidas Polk*, vol. II, 325.
119. Quoted in Polk, *Leonidas Polk*, vol. I, 328–29.
120. Quoted in Polk, *Leonidas Polk*, vol. I, 338.
121. Polk, *Leonidas Polk*, vol. I, 331.
122. Reprinted in Polk, *Leonidas Polk*, vol. I, 348.
123. Robins, *Bishop of the Old South*, 145.
124. At the outbreak of the Civil War, Albert Sidney Johnston was serving in the United States Army Department of the Pacific in California and resigned his Federal commission, returning to the Confederacy by July 1861.
125. Polk was referring to William Meade, third bishop of the Episcopal Diocese of Virginia.
126. Leonidas Polk to Stephen Elliott, 22 June 1861, Polk papers.
127. Sarah Dorsey to Leonidas Polk, 20 February 1862, Polk papers.
128. Green, *Memoir of Rt. Rev. James Hervey Otey*, 91.
129. Ibid., 101.
130. Polk, *Leonidas Polk*, vol. I, 362.
131. Ibid.

CHAPTER 6

132. Girardi, "Leonidas Polk," 1.
133. Robins, *Bishop of the Old South*, 150.
134. Baumer, *Not All Warriors*, 136.
135. Polk, *Leonidas Polk*, vol. II, 2–3.
136. Park, *General Leonidas Polk*, 173–74.
137. Polk, *Leonidas Polk*, vol. II, 5.
138. Eaton, *History of the Southern Confederacy*, 156.

139. Polk, *Leonidas Polk*, vol. II, 5.

140. United States War Department, *War of the Rebellion*, 315.

141. Stoker, *Grand Design*, 44.

142. Ibid., 47.

143. Leonidas Polk to LeRoy Pope Walker, 21 July 1861, Polk papers.

144. Leonidas Polk to LeRoy Pope Walker, 28 July 1861, Polk papers.

145. Polk, *Leonidas Polk*, vol. II, 13.

146. Leonidas Polk to Jefferson Davis, 29 August 1861, Polk papers.

147. Polk, *Leonidas Polk*, vol. II, 14.

148. Ibid., 15.

149. Ibid., 17–18.

150. Stoker, *Grand Design*, 49.

151. Polk, *Leonidas Polk*, vol. II, 19.

152. Leonidas Polk to Beriah Magoffin, 1 September 1861, Polk papers.

153. Polk, *Leonidas Polk*, vol. II, 21.

154. Leonidas Polk to Beriah Magoffin, 8 September 1861, Polk papers.

155. John M. Johnson to Leonidas Polk, 9 September 1861, Polk papers.

156. Leonidas Polk to John M. Johnson, 9 September 1861, Polk papers.

157. Polk, *Leonidas Polk*, vol. II, 25.

158. Lossing, *Pictorial History*, 75.

159. Jefferson Davis to Leonidas Polk, 15 September 1861, Polk papers.

160. Quoted in Polk, *Leonidas Polk*, vol. II, 28.

161. Polk, *Leonidas Polk*, vol. II, 36–37.

162. Stoker, *Grand Design*, 51.

163. Polk, *Leonidas Polk*, vol. II, 44.

164. Leonidas Polk to Frances Devereux Polk, 31 January 1861, Polk papers.

CHAPTER 7

165. United States War Department, *War of the Rebellion*, 300.

166. Cunningham, *Shiloh*, 140.

167. Polk, *Leonidas Polk*, vol. II, 103.

168. Leonidas Polk, Report of the Battle of Shiloh, Polk papers.

169. United States War Department, *War of the Rebellion*, 314.

170. Leonidas Polk to Frances Devereux Polk, 9 April 1862, Polk papers.

171. Robins, *Bishop of the Old South*, 169.

172. Ibid., 176.

173. Ibid., 178.

174. Foote, *Civil War*, 737.

175. Ibid., 739.

176. United States War Department, *War of the Rebellion*, 699.

177. Leonidas Polk to Frances Devereux Polk, 30 March 1863, Polk papers.

178. Leonidas Polk to Frances Devereux Polk, 11 April 1863, Polk papers.

179. Fremantle, *Three Months in the Southern States*, 139.

180. Ibid., 147.

181. Baumer, *Not All Warriors*, 139.

182. Fremantle, *Three Months in the Southern States*, 162.

183. Leonidas Polk to Frances Devereux Polk, 14 June 1863, Polk papers.

184. Robins, *Bishop of the Old South*, 180.

185. Leonidas Polk to Jefferson Davis, 6 October 1863, Polk papers.

186. Ibid.

187. Leonidas Polk to Jefferson Davis, 8 December 1863, Polk papers.

CHAPTER 8

188. McMurry, *Atlanta 1864*, xii.

189. Ibid., 13.

190. Ibid., 61.

191. Ibid., 62.

192. Polk, *Leonidas Polk*, vol. II, 370–71.

193. Ibid., 374.

194. Ibid.

195. Watkins, *Maury Grays*, 133.

196. General Joseph E. Johnston, General Field Order No. 2, 14 June 1864, Polk papers.

197. Downs, "Battle of Kennesaw Mountain," 1114.

198. Green, *Memoir of Rt. Rev. James Hervey Otey*, 109.

199. McPherson, *Abraham Lincoln*, 12.

BIBLIOGRAPHY

MANUSCRIPTS

Polk, Leonidas. Papers, University of North Carolina Library, Chapel Hill, NC.

BOOKS AND ARTICLES

Ambrose, Stephen E. *Duty, Honor, Country: A History of West Point*. Baltimore, MD: Johns Hopkins University Press, 1966.

Armentrout, Donald S. *James Hervey Otey: First Episcopal Bishop of Tennessee*. Knoxville: Episcopal Diocese of Tennessee, 1984.

Arnold, James. *Shiloh 1862: The Death of Innocence*. New York: Osprey Publishing, 1998.

Bacon, Leonard. *A History of American Christianity*. New York, 1921.

Baumer, William Henry. *Not All Warriors: Portraits of 19th Century West Pointers Who Gained Fame in Other Than Military Fields*. New York: Books for Libraries Press, 1971.

Boles, John B. *Masters and Slaves in the House of the Lord: Race and Religion in the American South, 1740–1870.* Lexington: University of Kentucky Press, 1990.

Butler, Diana Hochstedt. *Standing Against the Whirlwind: Evangelical Episcopalians in Nineteenth-Century America.* Oxford: University Press, 1995.

Carrigan, Jo Ann. "Impact of Yellow Fever on Life in Louisiana." *Louisiana History: A Journal of the Louisiana Historical Association* 4, no. 1 (1963): 15–26.

Chorley, Edward Clowes. *Men and Movements in the American Episcopal Church.* New York: Scribner, 1948.

Cunningham, O. Edward. *Shiloh and the Western Campaign of 1862.* Edited by Gary D. Joiner and Timothy Smith. New York: Savas Beatie, 2007.

Downs, Alan C. "Battle of Kennesaw Mountain." *Encyclopedia of the American Civil War: A Political, Social and Military History.* Edited by David S. Heidler and Jeanne Heidler. New York: W.W. Norton and Company, 2000.

Duffy, John. *The Rudolph Matas History of Medicine in Louisiana.* Baton Rouge, LA: Pelican Publishing, 1976.

Eaton, Clement. *A History of the Southern Confederacy.* New York: Simon and Schuster, 1965.

The Episcopal Church. *Episcopal Life.* September 2006.

———. *Journal of the Proceedings of the Bishops, Clergy, and Laity of the Protestant Episcopal Church in the United States of America.* Philadelphia: King and Baird, 1854, 1860.

Finklen, John, and Grace King. *A History of Louisiana.* New Orleans: L. Graham and Sons, 1893.

Follett, Richard. *The Sugar Masters: Planters and Slaves in Louisiana's Cane World, 1820–1860.* Baton Rouge: Louisiana State University Press, 2007.

Foote, Shelby. *The Civil War, A Narrative: Fort Sumter to Perryville.* New York: Random House, 1986.

Freehling, William W. *The Road to Disunion, Volume II: Secessionists Triumphant.* Oxford: University Press, 2007.

Fremantle, Arthur L. *Three Months in the Southern States: April–June, 1863.* Bedford, MA: Applewood Press, 1864.

Girardi, Robert I. "Leonidas Polk and the Fate of Kentucky in 1861." *Confederate Generals in the Western Theater: Essays on America's Civil War.* Edited by Lawrence Lee Hewitt and Arthur W. Bergeron. Series Editor Gary D. Joiner. Knoxville: University of Tennessee Press, 2011.

Green, William Mercer. *Memoir of Rt. Rev. James Hervey Otey.* New York, 1885.

Holmes, David L. *A Brief History of the Episcopal Church.* Harrisburg, PA: Trinity Press, 1993.

Lossing, Benson J. *A Pictorial History of the Civil War in the United States.* Hartford: Thomas Belknap, 1874.

Loveland, Anne C. *Emblem of Liberty: The Image of Lafayette in the American Mind.* Baton Rouge: Louisiana State University Press, 1971.

McIlvaine, Charles Pettit. *Memoirs of the Right Reverend Charles Pettit McIlvaine.* Edited by Reverend William Carus. New York: Thomas Whitaker, 1889.

McMurry, Richard M. *Atlanta 1864: Last Chance for the Confederacy.* Lincoln: University of Nebraska Press, 2000.

McPherson, James. *Abraham Lincoln and the Second American Revolution.* Oxford: University Press, 1991.

Otey, James Hervey. *Preaching the Gospel: A Charge Delivered to the Clergy of the Protestant Episcopal Church in the State of Tennessee.* Nashville: W.F. Bang and Company, 1840.

Parks, Joseph. *General Leonidas Polk, CSA: The Fighting Bishop.* Baton Rouge: Louisiana State University Press, 1962.

Perry, William Stevens. *Episcopate in America.* New York: Christian Literature Company, 1895.

Polk, William M. *Leonidas Polk: Bishop and General.* Vols. I and II. New York: Longmans, Green and Company, 1915.

Posey, Walter B. "The Protestant Episcopal Church: An American Adaptation." *Journal of Southern History* 25, no. 1 (1959): 7–11.

Robins, Glenn. *The Bishop of the Old South: The Ministry and Civil War Legacy of Leonidas Polk.* Macon, GA: Mercer University Press, 2006.

Southard, Samuel. "The Southern Soldier-Saint." *Journal for the Scientific Study of Religion* 8, no. 1 (1969): 39–46.

Stoker, Donald. *The Grand Design: Strategy and the United States Civil War.* Oxford: University Press, 2010.

Wall, Bennett H. *Louisiana: A History.* Wheeling, IL: Harlan Davidson, 1990.

Watkins, Pvt. Sam R. *Maury Grays, First Tennessee Regiment, or a Side Show of the Big Show.* Chattanooga, TN: Times Publishing, 1900.

Winters, John David. *The Civil War in Louisiana.* Baton Rouge: Louisiana State University Press, 1991.

Yeatman, Trezevant. "St. John's: A Plantation Church of the Old South." *Tennessee Historical Quarterly* (December 1951): 344–57.

GOVERNMENT DOCUMENTS

United States War Department. *The War of the Rebellion: Correspondence, Orders, Reports and Returns of the Union Authorities.* Harrisburg, PA: National Historical Society, 1971.

INDEX

A

Atlanta Campaign 102

B

Beauregard, P.G.T. 69, 78, 88
Book of Common Prayer 33, 56
Bragg, Braxton 88, 95
Buchanan, James 56, 58

C

Chattanooga, Battle of 93
Chickamauga, Battle of 81, 90
Confederate States of America 17, 19, 53

D

Davis, Jefferson 21, 27, 63, 66, 72, 73, 74, 77, 79, 87, 91, 93, 99, 102
Diocese of Louisiana 60, 66, 69

E

Elliott, Stephen 45, 46, 60, 63, 107
Episcopal Church 11

F

Fremont, John C. 71, 74

G

General Convention Episcopal Church 35, 36, 50, 52
Grant, Ulysses S. 77, 82, 99, 100
Great Awakening 46, 51

H

Hardee, William 82
Hood, John Q. 92

J

Johnston, Albert Sidney 27, 63, 69, 76, 77, 79, 82, 84
Johnston, Joseph 69, 92, 97

K

Kennesaw Mountain, Battle of 105

L

Lee, Robert E. 69
Lincoln, Abraham 57, 71, 73
lost cause 14, 100, 107

M

Magoffin, Beriah 74, 76
McIlvaine, Charles Pettit 27, 38, 50
Mississippi River 39, 43, 67, 71, 73, 78, 100
Moore, Thomas Overton 57

O

Otey, James Hervey 36, 51, 56, 66

P

Perryville, Battle of 19, 90
Pillow, Gideon 71, 74, 77
Pine Mountain 18, 102, 105
Pittsburg Landing 81
Polk, William Mecklenburg 11, 14, 104

R

Ravenscroft, John 25, 26
Rosecrans, William 93

S

Sherman, William T. 85
Shiloh, Battle of 81
Smith, Edmund Kirby 88

T

Thayer, Sylvanus 26
Thibodaux, Louisiana 14, 39, 45

U

University of the South 13, 18, 50

V

Virginia Theological Seminary 30

W

western theater, Civil War 67, 77, 81, 99
West Point Military Academy 13, 38
Whitefield, George 46
Wilson's Creek, Battle of 72

Y

yellow fever 41, 44

Z

Zollicoffer, Felix 70

ABOUT THE AUTHOR

Cheryl H. White, PhD, is a professor of history at Louisiana State University in Shreveport. Her research interests include medieval Europe, Tudor England and Christian/religious history. In addition to numerous journal articles and academic conference presentations, she has co-written two previous titles with The History Press, *Historic Haunts of Shreveport* and *Wicked Shreveport*.

Visit us at
www.historypress.net